BIG JOE EGAN

BIG JOE EGAN

THE TOUGHEST WHITE MAN ON THE PLANET

BY JOE EGAN

WITH

RANALD GRAHAM

FOREWORD BY

MIKE TYSON AND TOM PATTI

First published in hardback in Great Britain 2005
By Pennant Books
A division of Pennant Publishing Ltd

Text copyright © Joe Egan 2005

British Library Cataloguing-in-Publication Data:
A catalogue record for this book is available from
The British Library

ISBN 0-9550394-1-X

Design and typset by Envy Design Ltd

Printed and bound in Great Britain by
William Clowes Ltd, Beccles, Suffolk

*While every effort has been made to trace the relevant copyright-holder.
This has proved impossible in some cases and copyright-owners are
invited to contact the publishers.*

Some names in this book have been changed for legal reasons.

Pennant Books Ltd
A division of Pennant Publishing Ltd
PO Box 5071
Hove, BN52 9BB

I DEDICATE THIS BOOK TO MY MUM AND DAD WHO
HAVE STOOD BY ME THROUGH EVERYTHING.

THE MEN AND WOMEN THAT STOOD BESIDE MY
FAMILY DURING THE EVICTION.

I WOULD ALSO LIKE TO WISH BRIAN PETERS AND
RTE TELEVISION ALONG WITH ALL THE IRISH BOXERS
EVERY SUCCESS IN THE FUTURE AND ALL WHO
ARE DEDICATED TO THE SPORT I LOVE.

Contents

Acknowledgements

Ruth; My Life.

My dad Joe and my mum Ann who I thank for making me the man I am.

My brothers Emmet and Connolly along with my sisters Constance, Maureen, Ann and Sinéad.

Charlie Hale and Ken Purchase for encouraging me to write a book, also Cass Pennant and Laxley Pennant plus Ranald Graham for making it happen.

My amateur boxing trainers: Keith Drewitt, London. Paddy Hallett, Newcastle. Tony Mahon, Benny Bracken, both Donore Boxing Club. My professional trainers Paul McCullagh, John Breen, Bernardo Checa.

For all their help with my last fight and their friendship: Saleem 'Sal' Raza, Flex Fitness Gym, Digbeth. Christian Brady, Patrick and Paul Naughton, Cleary's pub, Digbeth. Darren Weston, Nigel Rafferty and Steve Petitt, Mark Williams, Mikey Pencheon, Dave Lovell.

For friendship and support in good and bad times: John and Sheila Delaney. The Hallett family, Newcastle. The Rock family, Dublin. John 'Boxer' Finn, Paddy Finn, Dubliner pub, Birmingham. Steve Dawson, Jim Moriarty, Martin Morgan, Alex Berry & family, Paul Howard. Gerard Gordon, Gary Peak. Tommy Byrne, Clive McNally, B.M.C. UK, Tony Southall & family, Paul and Adam Underhill, Tommy Scragg, Moya Payroll Services. Keith Lewis, Peter Leachman of Seconds Out Presents. McCullagh family, Belfast. Mike Higgins Speedy Hire. Gail Burke, Tom Casino, Showtime. Jay Bright, John 'Jobo' Dunleavy & family. Cathal and Leslie Ryan, Bruce Silverglade and Bob Jackson, Gleason's gym, New York. Peter O'Neil & family, Adam and Eve pub, Jim Brady, Red Wood Club, Birmingham. Iain McCallister of Man Commercial Protection Ltd. The Egans everywhere www.eganclan.org, my aunties, uncles, cousins, nephews and nieces (you know who you are). Mike Tyson, Tom Patti, Floyd Patterson, Steve Collins, Jim Rock, Barry McGuigan, Sean Mannion, Dave 'Boy' McAuley, Bunny Johnson. Ricky 'The Hitman' Hatton, Alan Minter, Ross Minter, Paul 'Silky' Jones, Danny McAlindon, Steve 'Hatter' McLaire, Total Fitness, Tamworth. Joe McGrail, Colin & Amy Stephens, John Murray, Dave Cowley, Stevie Rogerson, Dave Mitchell, Michael 'IKIE' Watson, Big Barry Fitzpatrick, Tommy Phoenix, Brian Peters, Howard Evans, SPV Road Carpet Ltd. Ken Pritchard, KLM Associates Accountants. Dean Wale, Kenny Norville, Chris Nurse, Tony 'Banger' Walsh. Tom Shanahan, Billy Shanahan, Warwick Ellis, Mark Peters, Mick Cooke, Les Allen. The owners and staff at

Acknowledgements

Manzils Indian restaurant. Ron Gray, Steve Gray, Dave 'Pitbull' Jennings, Frank Peters, John Lawlor, John O'Shea, Jack Doyle & family, Pulaski, New York. Joe and Barbara Gaffney, Syracuse, New York. Andy Lillis, Jason Dimmock, Phil Bell, Gerry Callan, Jimmy Magee, Dean Smith, Dan Lane, Rylane Boxing Club. Leo Lawlor, Shaun McCarron, Dan Curran, Fran Curran, Sean O'Regan, Patrick 'OZ' Corcoran. Mark McCarron, Ian Clarkson, John Rawlings, Joe Colgan, Mike Rowens, Clifton Mitchell, Tony Brooks, Kenny Rainford, Ray Fisher, Wally Dixon, Keith Walker, Kevin Sanders, the Lawlor family, Birmingham. Vince 'The Gloves' Smith, Bakshi Shemar, Scott Murray, Barsports. Martin 'Man Mountain' Snow. Bobby Burns & family. Gary Chin & family. Tommy Sullivan, Peggy O'Neills Bar, New York. Willie Cooney, Dean Twist, All at Heggarty's Gym, Dublin. Father Joe Drumgoole, Fergus Murray, Oliver Egan, Ken Harrington, Phil 'The Power' Taylor, Steve Arnold, Everyone in GTN Security UK, plus Chemical Nutritional Products Mr Kerry Kayes & Dorian Yates thank you both.

My heartfelt and most sincere thank you to a very special group of friends: Tommy McGeough, Warren Wiggan, Martin Morel, Steven Dalton, Katherine Dalton James Campbell, Gerard Campbell, Danny Brown, Tony 'GT' Bauld. Tony Williams, John McBean, Hugh 'Lurch' Taylor, Ronnie Thackeray, Noel Delaney R.I.P., Al Gavin R.I.P., Sean Moore R.I.P.

Pictures reproduced by kind permission of: Paul Howard, Alan Shaw, Jerry Hjelter, Tony Bowden, *The Belfast Telegraph*, Action Images

Foreword by Mike Tyson and Tom Patti

There is a point in our lives when we choose to become a man. Although some may avoid making this transition, deciding to become a boxer speeds that process up. For some, this is an option; for others, it's a true passion. Undoubtedly, being a fighter takes a certain type of character, one that requires a young boy to face his fears, accept loneliness and aspire to greatness. When any young man was invited to live and train with Cus d'Amato, he may not have known it, but he just chose the most demanding and rewarding experience a fighter could enjoy. As Cus would promptly tell you, 'You'll be judged by your actions, not your words.'

For years, different boys would come and go through the house of Cus d'Amato and Camille Ewald. Only a few had the discipline to sacrifice and endure the rigours of life in Catskill, NY. When Joe Egan came to live with us, we were curious if the Irish amateur champion had it in him. We found out that he did... and more. There were two levels of judgement: first, what is this person like to live with? Second, what does he have in him as a fighter?

In the beginning, Joe missed his family a great deal. We were all strangers to him and the testing period was under way. We didn't know if this guy was a short-timer or capable of hanging with those of us that had no other option but to be a fighter. Joe was a nice enough guy, quick to help around the house, doing the dishes and chores that Camille required all of the other boys to do. When he spoke of Ireland, he talked of its beautiful land and the lovely people back home. Now, we had never been to Ireland, but there is no doubt in our minds that the wizardry and speed of a leprechaun is nothing short of amazing. Joe's tales even had Camille (our mother) verifying the shenanigans of those mysterious little bastards.

The biggest test in the gym was when Joe climbed into the ring to box with me. Since he wasn't from the States, I didn't think that he would be intimidated by any sort of reputation that might have been out there about me. Just as I suspected, when the bell sounded, Joe came out to box. In countless sessions, many fighters would fight to survive or not fight at all. Joe fought with the skill and poise of an experienced fighter. No doubt, Irish fighters have guts. In fact, if you follow history, Joe represented true Irish fashion. He fought hard and gave all that he had.

One day, I walked into the room where Tommy Patti and Joe were hanging out. Joe was feeling down. I guess being this far away from home was starting to catch up with him.

We said, 'Look, man, we're your family now. You can't think about where you're not.' We couldn't let him dismiss the fact that he was part of our home. He'd come so far and proven himself; we couldn't let him leave just 'cause he was homesick. He stayed for as long as he could and one of our brothers he became.

Best of luck always, Joe
Your brothers Mike Tyson and Tom Patti

AUTHOR'S NOTE:
Irish heavyweight boxer Joe Egan has sparred with Mike Tyson, who never put him down and became a lifelong friend; he's boxed with Lennox Lewis; and he's shared a post-fight ambulance with Raging Bull Jake La Motta... this is Joe's story as he tells it himself.

Prologue

To stand in front of a gun for me, to run at a man that was aiming a gun at me, was the greatest act of courage I have ever seen.

When I saw Jake Welch step towards me with the shotgun levelled, I actually hid. I got a fright and I jumped back and hid behind the wall. And I'm not ashamed to say I was scared.

As you enter the front doors, you turn to the left into the lounge, and go straight on into the bar – just to the right is the wall that I hid behind.

And, as Jake Welch stood there, preparing to shoot, while people were screaming and diving for cover, Steve Dalton ran out.

Jake Welch didn't expect an unarmed man would run at him. He was startled and he turned and jumped back himself. As he jumped back, he fired the shotgun half downward, at point-blank range. The blast hit the ground, and bounced up, most of it then hitting Dalton who was knocked off his feet.

The lads were pulling the pellets out of him for hours.

He wouldn't go to the hospital.

Afterwards, I said to Steve, 'That's the bravest thing I've ever seen in my life.'

He said, 'Joe, it was madness.'

'Steve, thank you very much.'

'I didn't do it for you. My wife Tina and my sister Cathy was in the pub. If those animals had got in, they would have butchered them. I did it for them.'

'Steve, I don't care who you did it for, as far as I'm concerned, you did it for me. Thank you.'

CHAPTER ONE

Ringsend Boy

I'm the eldest of seven kids. I've got four sisters and two brothers. My dad worked on a building site, as a concrete worker. My mum was a housewife. My father always worked in England, and he spent a lot of years working as a subcontractor on the building sites, so during the summer holidays from school we used to go over there and I'd spend seven to eight weeks over there at a time, sometimes longer. That's how I started boxing, when I joined a boxing club there at the age of 10 – Earlsfield Amateur Boxing Club.

We used to move back and fore as kids, wherever my dad was working. We were over there, back in Ireland, over there again. It was a difficult time for my parents because the work was in England for my dad. When I was only eight or nine, my dad was working in Manchester, and we lived in Newton Heath, and because we had the

Irish accent I got bullied and my two front teeth knocked out. Never liked bullies, still don't like bullies to this day.

My dad used to show me and my brother a straight left in the back garden. He used to go, straight left, straight left. My dad boxed, not at a great level, but he boxed. As an amateur, he used to box with the Corinthians Club in Dublin. Maxie McCullagh, European gold medallist in 1947, was his old trainer.

My mum used to do this stew. Stew was a big thing, was stew. Every day through the week, it didn't matter, but you had to be at the dinner table on a Sunday. And, if you weren't at the dinner table on a Sunday, there was hell to pay with everyone waiting to eat until you're all at the table.

Ringsend. That's where I'm from in Dublin. When I was a kid, I went to Star of the Sea Primary School. When I was about seven or eight, I fell and split my head open. It was in the playground. I was running along and my sandal strap broke. I tripped and fell into the iron railings. I stood up, wasn't aware of any blood or anything, and just carried on playing. Then I became aware of all the kids screaming and pointing at me. The cut was all the way from the forehead to the middle of my head. I felt it, and it was so deep my fingers went right inside.

The paramedics were amazed that I was able to walk from the playground to the ambulance, and from the ambulance into the hospital, where I had 23 stitches put in. It was a real talking point. I was even nicknamed 'knucklehead' for a while.

But it proved, even at that age, I could take a punch!

Then I moved up to Ringsend School, on the docks.

My dad used to go to the docks. The boats used to put in at the docks, the Polish coal boats. And you could go down, and you could get 20 pints of Polish beer for £6 Irish and in English money they did it for £4. And you'd get a bottle of vodka for £2.50 – the Polish vodka would blow the head off you.

My dad used to have the poker game on a Thursday night. There was Macker O'Conner, Mattie Dunphy, Joe Drumgoole; Brian Murray used to come, and Father Oliver Egan. Ken Harrington the police officer came over too. We used to wait until they got drunk and they'd drop money on the floor. I used to clean up. I'd always get some – only 10p and 20p and 50p and stuff that had dropped on the floor, but that was great.

One evening, Matty Dunphy stood up, twisted drunk, and he said to my dad, who's also called Joe, 'Joe, I'll knock your house down.'

So my dad – he was twisted as well – says, 'Go on then, Matty, knock the house down.'

So he did this mad running kick at the wall, kicked the wall and he fell down. And you could see the leg was shattered. I swear to God the leg swelled up in the jeans. So he stood up – you could see the pain in his face, but he was that drunk he didn't realise – and he said, 'Joe, I won't knock your house down, otherwise you'll have nowhere to live.' And he walked out. This was about half-four in the morning.

The next day we're up maybe half-eight, nine o'clock to pick up the coins that had dropped on the floor. Then we said we're going to check on Matty. So me and my brother went round to Matty's house. He was still living with his mother. We knocked on the door. Mrs Murphy opened the door.

'Hello, Mrs Murphy, is Matty in?'

'No,' she said, 'he went out for a game of cards, he never came back.'

So we said we'll have a look around for him. So we're looking around. He's fallen into a garden and he's asleep in the front of the garden. So me and my brother just phoned an ambulance because there's no point in trying to attend to him. And we waited until the ambulance came. He'd broken his leg in three places, shattered the leg. The ankle, the knee and the hip or whatever. The leg was smashed. But the jeans had kept the swelling from going too far. He'd given the wall a right kick. It wasn't even a row, it was just full-of-drink madness.

My nan used to have a grocery shop at the front, and in the lane she had the back shop, which was the fruit and vegetable shop. Opposite my grandmother's back shop was Mrs Holmes's butcher's – she used to sell the pork. At the front, there was Farrelly's, which was the main butcher's for the steaks and stuff like that, but this was the pork shop in the lane.

There was a big lad used to deliver the meat, the pork, on one of them big old butcher's bikes. He used to come out of the butcher's shop and, instead of wheeling the bike up the hill, he used to get on to the bike to cycle it. It's the easiest way to get to the top of the hill, right. He'd be cycling the bike up the hill and his arse used to be hanging out of his trousers.

Me and my brother – I was about 11 or 12 – got this big leather belt. The butcher's lad would come by on the bike, and we'd jump out, whack him with a belt, hit him across the backside, turn and run, hell for leather. We'd be laughing!

Anyway, this particular day, we did it once too often. I was at the side, crouched, ready to spring. As I jumped out, he threw the bike on the ground because he was ready for us – he was already half off the bike. He threw the bike on the ground, and he turned. And, I tell you, I turned at the same time he turned. The fear! His hands came down the back of my neck, just missed me. If he'd caught me, he would have kicked 10 sorts of shit out of me. And I ran! I ran as fast as my legs would take me. My brother was gone, he was gone like a whippet. I tell you, we never did that again.

Me and my brother were in the sea scouts because my dad encouraged us to do lots of things just to stay off the streets. We also joined the St John Ambulance Brigade. We used to row with the sea scouts. I was in 4th Port Dodder Sea Scouts – from the Dodder canal, which runs through Dublin. The first port was Ringsend and, although I was from Ringsend, the Ringsend troop was too full. So I joined the 4th Port Dodder. Me and my brother were in the same rowing crew. John Allen was the cox, Dermot Murray was the stroke, I was the second stroke, my brother was second bow and Frank Sheen was the bow. That was the four crew. We won the Wood Latimer Cup, which is the oldest rowing cup in Ireland. We won that in Malahide. I had some great years in the sea scouts.

My nan used to drink in a pub called Clark's pub and they used to have a room where all the old dears used to have a drink. And they used to call it the diddy room. And all the 'old 'uns' used to drink in there. So, after me and my brother used to box and win or lose, we used to have to bring our trophies down and show my nan. And we used to go to other different pubs and different people would give you a pound, 50p. You'd get a bit of a collection together. We were only kids. But they used to bring us into the diddy room, and all the old dears used to go, 'Oh look, give us a kiss,' and they'd be pulling me and they'd all try to kiss you. Of course, they were all pissed drunk. When you're a kid, you're thinking, 'Oh no.' But you come out, you made a few bob. And my mum used to insist on us going because she was proud of us and she used to bring us round. We didn't mind going to the other pubs, they'd say, 'Oh, well done, you lost or you won, well done,' and give you 50p. It was my nan's hometown, there was all my aunts and uncles and all their friends, my mum and dad's friends and we had a bit of a collection. But the last one was the diddy room. Oh, Jesus. You'd have more bruises coming out of there than you would from the fight because all these old dears grabbed at you, squeezing your arse and everything. It was funny.

My mum only ever hit me once. And what I was after doing was throwing stones. I didn't think it was bad what I'd done. And she came out and I was with a load of my friends, six or seven of my friends, and she had the tennis racket and she give me a whack with it. I was embarrassed getting hit in front of my friends so I wouldn't cry, I just wouldn't cry. And I looked at my friends like I'm a tough guy. And, because I was goading her on then, she hit me again. And I looked at my friends – no, it's not hurting me, but it was killing me. Anyway, she was like McEnroe with the tennis racket. She took lumps out of me with it. She couldn't hit me with her hands – it would have hurt her hands.

After a good few whacks, she was tired of hitting me, and the tennis racket was all bent up, and she went off crying, 'You're no good to me.'

So I looked at my friends, like, all macho, I haven't cried – I've took the beating and I haven't cried. Then my friends went off. As soon as they were round the corner, boy, I was in agony. And I went upstairs to bed with bruises, cuts and lumps out of me.

After a while, my mum came up. She felt really bad that she was having to hit me, because she'd never hit me before and she's never hit me since. And she was so upset that she came up. Anyway, with big hugs and kissing, she said, 'Are you all right?'

'Yeah.'

'Why didn't you cry after the first whack?'

If I'd have cried after the first whack, she'd have stopped. I was too proud to cry in front of my friends. I'm not saying that I don't cry – I've cried loads of times, but sometimes you bottle it up till you're on your own.

Both my parents have been a good guiding light. My dad always instilled discipline. He's raised a good family, he's been a hard-working man. My mum made sure none of us has gone hungry. My brothers and sisters, we were brought up well.

At that time when I was boxing as a kid, I always had great confidence in myself, I always felt a winner. I was very heavy – over 10 stone. I'd had a couple of fights in England – I boxed a kid from Battersea, Michael Simmons, fought him a couple of times. And I fought a guy called Robert Parker a couple of times. So I'd had like five or six fights in England from the age of 10–12.

So I've come home to Ireland and for my first fight in Ireland I was boxing with the Donore Boxing Club. I'd come up to the club and they said, 'You're boxing Sunday afternoon at the Phoenix Boxing Club at the back of Ryan's Barbers.'

I asked Tony Mahon, my trainer, 'Who am I boxing?'

He said, 'You're boxing a novice. The guy doesn't have any fight in him.'

At that stage, I'd had several fights. Nothing great, they're only kids. So I thought, 'Well, I should be able to beat him handy enough, I've had five or six fights.' Showing great confidence, but I was scared on the inside.

When I arrived at the Phoenix Boxing Club, there was a friend of mine there, a guy called Skinner Evans from Ringsend – the same town as me in Dublin – but he was boxing with the Phoenix Boxing Club. He was with this other fella. And I looked heavy. And Skinner goes, 'Hey there, Joe. Are you boxing?'

'Hello, Skinner. Yeah, I'm boxing some novice,' I said. 'I'll knock him out.'

So Skinner said, 'Oh great, good luck to you.'

So I said to the other fella with Skinner, 'Are you boxing as well?'

He said, 'Yeah.' He just looked an average – even though I was a kid, I looked heavy.

So I said, 'Good luck to you.'

'I don't need luck; I'm going to knock my fella out.'

So, next of all, I'm in the ring. I'm looking across the far side of the ring. I've seen that face before. It was the man I'd met outside with Skinner Evans. But he looked smaller than me because I was heavy and it turned out it was Steve Collins!

But at the time he was a year older (he still is a year older than me!) but at that age, when you're 12–13, a year makes a big difference. The fight referee's a guy called Lugs Brannigan, he's a legend in Dublin, an ex-Garda officer. A one-man riot squad. We used to call him Lugs because of his ears. This is my first experience of Lugs, my first experience of boxing in Ireland. And it starts off with Steven Collins giving me a right good pasting throughout that first round.

So I go back to the corner and Tony my trainer says, 'I'm going to retire you.'

I says, 'No, no, don't retire me, don't retire me! The referee will stop it if I'm getting too badly hurt. Let the referee stop it.' It's not as embarrassing getting stopped by the referee as throwing the towel in. And referees should not let you get pasted.

So I've gone back out for round two. What I didn't realise was Lugs thought everybody that was boxing was as tough as him!

I learned a hard lesson the hard way. Steve Collins pounded me to a pulp. I lost on points, but I went the distance. I cried for weeks, and we became great friends afterwards.

I boxed him years later at the Youth Championships but I was that bit older, a bit more experienced, where a year didn't make that much difference. And he went down then from heavyweight to light heavyweight and then down to middleweight.

I have a running joke about it with Steve because a couple of times in recent years I've done functions with him. Steve says, 'We boxed once,' and I say, 'No, Steve, we boxed twice. I hit you that hard in the second fight you don't remember it.' But he's been a good friend over the years. More credit to him for what he achieved, in becoming WBO middleweight champion.

He's always had a great boxing pedigree. It's in his family. His uncles were great boxers. The Collins family are well known in Dublin for the boxing and for the football, and they're well respected in boxing circles.

I was struggling to get fights when I was a kid because they're strict on the age and the weight when you're a kid. So I didn't start to get many fights until I was 16–17 and then at that stage I was thrown in with the men. So I hadn't served much of an apprenticeship in the boxing and suddenly I'm at a senior level. But I done well – I won four senior titles, two under-19 titles and a junior. I won the under-19s, the junior and the senior in one year.

I loved boxing. Wherever I could get a fight I'd set up home. I had a good fight once in Newcastle – I set up home in Newcastle. I went away with the North-East Division's team to box in Denmark. The guy over in Denmark, Morgens Palle, said he'd get me fights so I stayed over there too.

I just loved to fight. Win, lose or draw. I don't drink, I don't smoke. I didn't really enjoy the running! I wasn't really mad keen on the running. I would jog along at my own speed, walking pace, did the odd sprint. But in the gym – I used to love the gym, punch the bag, do the pads, and spar.

CHAPTER TWO

Tyson

CATSKILLS MOUNTAIN SOUP

I met boxing legend and three-times Heavyweight Champion Floyd Patterson on one of my trips with the Irish team to box in America. I was only young, just 17. We'd gone over at the end of '83, beginning of '84, and Floyd gave us the opportunity because he was married to an Irish lady – any of the Irish lads that wanted to stay, we'd be made welcome, he'd look after us.

It was through Floyd that I met the legendary cutsmen, Al Gavin and Bob Jackson. Floyd introduced me to them and they looked after me when I was in the States. They got me my sparring; I was sparring with different fighters every day so it was through them that I got to go to the Catskills. They'd contacted Cus and they said to him that they had a young up-and-coming heavyweight that was able to hold his own and that he could be a good sparring partner for some new heavyweight he was grooming called Mike Tyson.

I got a lift up to the Catskills from Bob Jackson. Driving up into the mountains was fantastic. The gym is above the police station in the main street of Catskill, but the house is about four or five miles outside the town. So, when we're driving up, we drive over a bridge – it's called Rip Van Winkle Bridge, after the legendary fictional character who slept for 40 years or something. Maybe because the Catskills is so peaceful and tranquil! There's the Irish part of the Catskills and the German part, from when the immigrants came over first. It's really, really beautiful.

So we drive up to the house and it's a big long drive to this magnificent white house. It was brick with wooden lattes over it, the white wooden lattes with the porch. It was like something that you'd see in a picture postcard – it was just magnificent, up on its own, in the mountains, and you could see the Hudson River at the bottom.

Camille, Cus d'Amato's sister-in-law, owned the house and Cus had set up this boxing camp. He had his fighters stay in this magnificent mansion! When we got there that afternoon, Al and Bob had a chat with Cus and they went on their way.

They took me to my room. It was a fantastic, fabulous house. It was like a huge hotel – it's the only way you could describe it.

Mike had been told that there was an Irish heavyweight coming up to spar with him. I didn't know who Mike was at the time. He'd only just gone professional. He'd been beaten in the American trials by Henry Tillman who then got the Olympic gold in the '84 Olympics. Mike had been getting rave reviews, and had signed pro with the legendary Cus d'Amato. But I wasn't aware of any of this. I'd just come over from Ireland, and I didn't even know who this guy Cus d'Amato was!

That evening, we all sat down together at the meal, in a room just off from the kitchen. Because the house was so big, there was like a breakfast part off from the kitchen. There was the kitchen, a big long breakfast bar and there was this long table.

Cus was at the head of the table, and the ladies Camille and Marnie were serving up the food. I was sitting at the table, and I was still a little bit shy. I've come to this new training camp, and, even though the reception was so warm, I felt a little unsure, and it was my first meal in this new environment. Camille had done the starter, which was the soup. And we grew up on stew at home in Ireland, so it was Camille's version of what I'd call a stew, it was a broth.

I was sitting to the right of Cus. There was Jay Bright, and another couple of sparring partners. Mike was sitting next to the two empty chairs where Camille and Marnie, who were doing the serving up, would be sitting. Up from me were the two Hilton boys – brothers from Canada – and Tom Patti and Mike.

So the food was served up. Cus said a few words, welcoming me to the table. And it was lovely; it was like something you'd see in a wonderful movie. It's hard to put into words, because I was made so welcome.

And so I'm eating the soup. I'm still a little bit shy, still getting used to it. And I thought, 'Do I speak when they're eating or not?' Because they're all eating and I didn't know what was the routine, what was their rules of the table. Different households have different rules. When we were kids, my dad didn't let us have elbows on the table. 'Get your elbows off the table! And don't talk when you're eating!' Things like that. Anyway, there's nothing been said, everyone's just eating their soup. And I thought, 'Well I'll compliment them on the stew.' It was a beautiful soup, it was lovely. So I said to Camille, after having the soup, 'That's a gorgeous soup!'

Cus looked up and everyone sort of stopped. Everyone was looking, so I thought, 'What have I said wrong? I'm a teenager, I've said something wrong!' And I'm just looking at Cus.

Finally, Cus says, 'Do you know something? I've often heard of a woman being called gorgeous, but never a soup!'

Then he started laughing, and everybody started laughing, so I started laughing and it was the ice broken. And I knew then that they were my kind of people. Even though I'd had the warm reception and they were lovely people, I now knew they were people that enjoyed a sense of humour. Even though it was a serious business, and boxing was a very, very serious business, and they had the potentially greatest heavyweight champion of the world sitting at the table, grooming him and training him, it was still so laid-back and humorous and friendly.

Cus had a wonderful laugh, a hearty laugh. It wasn't like ha-ha-ha, it was a proper hearty laugh. And the way he said it, Tom and Mike, we still talk about it now.

That first evening broke down any inhibitions that I

had, any doubts that I had that these people were as lovely as they came across and more. I loved Cus, I loved Camille, I loved Marnie, I loved Mike, I loved Tom, I loved Jay. It became a family bond.

So now the ice is broken and everybody's laughing and I feel ever so comfortable in the environment. I was just made to feel – actually, it's hard to put into words how I was made to feel. It was just fantastic.

Later that evening, we talked about boxing. Cus was talking about the history of Irish fighters. He was talking to me about different fighters and Mike was talking about different Irish fighters over the years. Rinty Monaghan, Gerry Cooney, all the different Irish fighters. Sean Mannion was after giving a great account of himself going 15 rounds in Madison Square Garden with Mike 'Body Snatcher' McCallum for the WBA middleweight title. Sean Mannion was a topic. Mike knew all about these fighters.

Then Barry McGuigan was mentioned. And Mike lit up. At the time, Barry was the new man from Ireland. He was the European champion and the British champion. He was the one they were raving about, he was the one getting rave reviews in America. And I knew about Barry, being Irish, and Mike idolised Barry McGuigan. I came alive then. I was able to talk to Mike. He was hanging on every word I spoke. I could have said anything – once I was speaking about Barry McGuigan, Mike was just Barry, Barry, Barry.

Mike loved the way he fought; he loved the aggression that he brought into the ring, his style of fighting. He loved the relationship that Barry had with Barney

Eastwood because it was similar to the relationship that Mike had with Cus. I know Barry and Mr Eastwood went their separate ways towards the end – for whatever reason, that's their own business – but at that time it was a warm manager/boxer, father/son relationship. And Mike related to that with Cus d'Amato in the manager and the father figure, who went on to be his stepfather. And he'd seen how every time Barry was interviewed on the television with Mr Eastwood, there was the embrace, there was the hug, it was more than a manager/fighter, it was a father/son, even though it wasn't a blood father/son. And that touched everybody at the time Eastwood and McGuigan were going to the top, the warmth of the relationship that they had. You don't see it with fighter/managers now because it's business. This was more than business and Mike related to that. And it was lovely.

So it was through Barry McGuigan first of all that me and Mike became the close friends that we became. That first night, when Barry McGuigan was mentioned we suddenly had a bond straight away.

The next morning, there was six of us went out jogging. The first mile was just a nice pace. I thought, 'This will do me, it's a nice jogging pace.' Next of all, some of the lads are saying, 'Right, that's the warm-up jog done, let's start on the speeding.'

Whoosh, Mike was gone! I couldn't believe it. No other fighters could stick with him on the run; he can run, a great runner. You couldn't see him for dust – whoosh, gone.

I did about four miles, five miles, at my pace. I wasn't

the greatest of runners; I never liked to run that much but I did it because it was a necessity for boxing. You have to do running for stamina. But I had my own sort of slowish pace.

I was about 14 stone 10 to 15 stone. Mike would have been around the same weight – 15.5, 15.6, 15 and a half stone. He was a solid man, but he could run. I used to jog, but Mike was like a gazelle.

After that first run, we came back, showered up, had our breakfast. I remember Mike eating loads of sausages with red sauce. I couldn't believe it. He'd have a plate of sausages, honest to God, just a massive plate of sausages. I thought to myself, 'He's got an appetite, he's got a great appetite.'

So anyway, I went for a little bit of a lie down, a bit of a rest. Then I got up and was taken in the minibus to the gym which was in the main street, Catskill, above the police station.

The gym was a big open space with the ring against the stage, and four or five big bags. On the stage, there was like a sandbag on a rope that they used to push at Mike and he used to slip like it was a punch coming at him. It was lovely to watch, beautiful to watch him training.

I did a bit of bag work. I saw him doing neck exercises. He put his head in a towel and arched his back – like the way the gymnasts do the crab but without the hands, just roll on his neck. He had what's known as a stovepipe neck where your neck is wider than your head. He had a 19in neck, so you can say a 20in neck, but his head might have only been 18in. So he had this massive neck. And I watched him doing the exercises. Unbelievable. And the balance that he had doing them. Watching him train was a treat in itself.

I was watching him sparring and I could see the moves, and I thought, 'He's good, like, there's no taking away from him, he's good.' He's landing some powerful shots on these sparring partners. I wasn't to spar with him until the following day. But I wasn't afraid. I still didn't realise at the time who he was and what they expected of him.

So I watched him skipping. He was brilliant. He'd mesmerise you with a skipping rope. It was beautiful. It was just lovely to see the man with the skipping rope. He was unbelievable. Such gracefulness and rhythm for a powerful man, beautiful.

Anyway, we all went back, had a bit of a rest, had the evening meal, and then we went for a walk. Me and Mike and Cus, and whoever walked with us that night. Walked and talked. And talked about the next day's sparring.

Cus was saying, 'Look, you'll be wearing big gloves and you'll have headgear on, but, if at any time through the sparring you feel that you don't want to go on, don't feel that you've got to impress anybody here. Just use it as a learning, you're learning.'

Some of the sparring partners were journeymen fighters that had done their best as pro fighters, and now they were sparring partners; they were in the sparring partner mould. I was still a young man that was going to learn. I wasn't there to be cannon fodder.

Cus d'Amato took an interest in me the same as he took an interest in all his fighters. I wasn't there just to be a punchbag for Mike Tyson. There was no fighter there that wasn't given the warmth and the reception that I was given. We were all given the same warmth. And, of course, at the same time he ran the camp, a training camp, a boxing camp. So it wasn't just one fighter in Mike Tyson. He had other fighters, and he had an interest in them all.

MY FIRST SPAR WITH TYSON

I'll never forget the first shot Mike hit me with. It was a straight right to the body that caught me round the back. I turned side on, and he caught me on the hipbone. And I know myself my feet came off the canvas; I know he lifted me with that punch. But, luckily enough, it didn't catch me straight on, he caught me at the side. God, I could feel the power in the punch. I'd seen it the day before, but, until you actually feel it, you know feeling is believing!

I thought to myself, 'I'm not going to drop my guard with this fella, that's for sure.' So I'm sparring and holding on. I won't say trying to survive, but trying to cushion the blows of his punches. Smother him, lean on him, do different things. And at the end of the first round, I thought to myself, 'Well, I've done one round anyway, I've done all right.' Cus was there giving instructions. Kevin Rooney was the trainer there at the time. So, they wet me down, chuck me out, do the round robin, put another man in.

That particular day, there was three of us. Me and two professional heavyweights. One of them had actually fought Frank Bruno.

You do one round of sparring, then you get out and the

next man gets in with Mike, so Mike was staying in there, but he was getting a fresh man every time. So that was my first round over. I got out, and the next guy got in. He did his three minutes, then he got out and the next guy got in; he did his three minutes, then he got out, and then it was my turn to come back in again. So Mike was now on his fourth round and it was only my second round. And, while he was getting them fresh, you had time to get your breath and talk to Cus, watch the sparring, and just get your composure again.

So I did my two rounds with Mike that first day and I was hurt, I was bruised. And we'd come back to the house and I'd gone and done the distance with him for what I was to do. Mike did six/eight rounds of sparring that day. I'd done the two rounds and I'd done OK.

I didn't spar the following day, but I sparred the day after that. I did two more rounds with him. Then, over a period of months, sometimes I'd do up to three rounds with him. Not one after the other, always the round robin, which was the sparring routine they were working. And he never put me down. He hurt me on a number of occasions, but it got to the stage then that I was afraid to try a combination because you wouldn't want to drop your guard, drop your hands for any split second because Mike was so fast, so you were throwing one punch and getting your guard back up as quick as you could.

One day Mike had really gone to town on all the sparring partners. Cus used to say what Mike lacks in experience he uses in aggression. And he was an aggressive type of fighter. He was aggressive in the sparring, he was aggressive in his training and he was aggressive in his actual fighting. But away from the training, away from the sparring, away from the fighting, the guy was a lovely man. As humble and as dignified a man as I've met in my life. I loved the man as a friend. I think the world of him. I can't sing his praises enough.

He had moods. In the sparring, on different days you have your good days and your bad days, and this particular day he was on top form and sent the message. He's a human being; some days you go to the gym, you're a bit stale; other days you go... you've probably seen it in the football, they're winning one day, the next day they can't even get the ball. It's the same in boxing – certain days Mike was on top of his game; other days he might be tired, a bit lethargic. This day he wasn't, he was in destructive form.

So, this particular day, I'll never forget it, he pounded his sparring partner to a pulp and in the end the guy said, 'I can get $10,000 for a fight and not take this much punishment! I don't need this!' and he started shouting at Cus.

Kevin had to jump in to stop Mike because Mike thought that Cus was being threatened by the fact that this guy was shouting, and the rage had come out then. The guy was shouting because he'd been getting battered and, in that particular round, his emotions had taken over. Mike came over sort of protective. But Kevin really pacified things. The sparring partner had been pounded and he wasn't happy with the way he had been smashed about. Kevin got him out of the ring. After that, he took off and went back to whatever state he was from.

But the sparring session continued!

I didn't go in next; one of the other sparring partners went in next, and he's given him a pasting too.

So you're sitting on the side of the stage there and there was the ring, and you're looking. And really you're like lambs going to the slaughter when he's on top form. You don't want to be next!

Cus used to just point at the different guys to be coming in or Kevin would point. And you're just sitting there, you're thinking to yourself, 'Jesus Christ.' You're looking at this guy who is getting pounded and you're thinking to yourself, 'This is all ahead of me.'

It wasn't just the power – it was the speed he delivered the punches at. And it was a completely different man in that ring; even in three minutes, he was a completely different man. This was a ferocious man within three minutes. Sheer ferocity that's what you can just put it down to. Raw green power coming at you.

He had so much skill, but people didn't give him the credit for the skill that he had. The moving of the head – it was hard to hit him. As soon as you threw a punch at him, he was moving. The reflexes he had were like a cat. And the power, the angles that he used to get the uppercuts to. Bigger men than me, more experienced than me, were getting hurt. And you could see and you could hear bone-crunching punches. And you're looking at this and you're sitting there, and harder men would flinch watching. And he wouldn't let up until Cus or Kevin said, that's it or the bell went; he would not let up.

After this particular session, I went up to my bedroom

and I had a cry. My side was very, very painful and swollen up. I was crying because I was in agony from the sparring session. I'm not ashamed to say I was crying. I was in pain, because he really did a turn on me.

And they were giving me the shout for something, to go for a walk or the call to come down for dinner, or whatever, and I didn't appear.

There was a knock on my door. It was Mike and Tom and Jay come to see how I was. 'Look, are you all right?' Because there was a great camaraderie there in the house, great friendship. And I was crying. So Mike thought I was homesick.

'It's all right,' he said, 'you miss your family.'

I thought to myself, 'I'm in agony because you're bashing me to a pulp.'

I was not homesick, but it just showed his lovely way. He wasn't thinking, 'I've just smashed you to bits and you're crying because I've smashed you to bits.' He'd switched off. He smashed me to a pulp. I'd done three rounds with him that day, nine minutes of the round robin. But, as far as he was concerned, I was man enough to take it. He wasn't going to rub it in. That wasn't him. I'm sure, in the back of his mind, if he was to sit back and think about it, he'd say, 'Well, he's crying because I've hurt him.' But he didn't want to add insult to injury. Instead, he said, 'You're homesick for your family; we're your family now.'

And it was lovely. And that's why I have the affection for him. I was crying because I was in pain from the sparring, but there was no gloating, there was no I'm the king of the ring, none of that. At that time in his early career, you couldn't see a weakness, you could not see a chink in his armour.

I walked down the main street and bought 10 Catskills postcards for $2 and posted them all to family and friends. I wrote exactly the same on each of the postcards: 'I am training along with the future heavyweight champion of the world, Mike Tyson!'

IRISH SHORTS!

I never went to his first fight. His pro debut was around March 1985. I think his second fight would have been in April some time. I was at his second and third pro fights and I sparred with him for those fights. I sparred with him for a number of other fights. But, at these particular fights, I was ever so proud because he boxed in my shorts.

Most of the times after a fight was stopped, Mike didn't stand over his opponent – he didn't gloat, he was dignified in victory.

When you box for your country, you're given the strip that you box in to keep, they're yours. But nine times out of ten, you might swap the vest with your opponent. I swapped a couple of vests, but not the shorts – no one swaps the shorts, it's the same as the soccer players, they swap their shirts, but not their shorts.

Me and Mike hadn't fought each other, but we'd sparred and we just thought it was a nice gesture and we swapped shorts. Mike's given me his international American shorts – I still have his American shorts when he fought for America – and I swapped him my Irish shorts. And Mike boxed two of his professional fights in my Irish shorts, in the white and green. I've had loads of people say to me – those of the Irish fighters that recognise the shorts – they were my shorts. So Mike fought two of his earliest amateur fights in my Irish international shorts. You can see them on the videos, Mike in the white and green.

They were my shorts!

THE PIGEON LOFT

I was away when he had his first pro fight in March 1985, because I'd gone home to Ireland for the Irish championships, which were always held around St Patrick's Day. So I wasn't there the day he signed his professional papers. As soon as I returned (after losing a controversial decision to Bernie Deasy), Mike brought me over to the garage to show me the gift that he was given by Jim Jacobs and Bill Cayton as a signing-on present – a magnificent brand-new Rolls-Royce Corniche. He hadn't achieved anything yet as a pro, this was just a gift. These are multi-millionaires, businessmen, and they were Cus's and Mike's friends.

Mike had a fascination with cars, but he also had a fascination with pigeons. Now I knew different pigeon fanciers in Ireland. Pigeons in Ireland was a big thing. So we spoke about the pigeons. Mike wasn't into the racing pigeons, he was into the tippler pigeons, Birmingham Roller pigeons; they stay up, and it's the endurance more than the race.

'You've not got a loft?' I asked.

'No,' he said.

So I said, 'We'll build a loft.' Not that I was much of a builder but the enthusiasm was there, and he had the same enthusiasm that I had.

So, in the yard, in the grounds of the house, right more or less at the front of the house down by the road, we built this pigeon loft. And it was a magnificent structure! To anybody with any building knowledge, it was probably a ramshackle shed really, but we built it and we put up the sign: TYSON'S FLYERS! It was lovely. And we were proud of it, and we had a bit of fun.

The funny thing is Mike had a fascination with pigeons and Camille had a fascination with cats.

She'd all little ornaments and stuff around the house of figurines of her cats. She was a Ukrainian lady, Camille. I used to send her stuff – you know little cats, this and that – when I was away, or when I came back I'd bring her a little present of cat stuff.

She loved Mike as his stepmum and he loved Camille, but the animals that they loved were arch enemies!

BOXING CLEVER

I watched hundreds of old fight films on the old cine reels upstairs in the Catskills. The whole top of the house was Mike's. His room was the whole top of this magnificent old-style mansion house. There were two adjacent rooms. Sometimes sparring partners might use them if the house was full – there was a lot of bedrooms in this house. Mike had an exercise bike upstairs and he used to sit on this bike and cycle and watch these old cine films. Jim Jacobs, his manager, had the biggest collection of fight footage in the world and Mike had access to the biggest library of boxing in the world. He had his own collection, but he also had access to Jim's collection. And Mike is passionate about boxing – if they were to put him on to *Mastermind* with the history of boxing as his chosen subject, there's nothing that Mike Tyson doesn't know about the history of boxing.

The man is passionate about boxing. And I just hope – and I really do mean this – I hope that the way he's been treated by the Boxing Association hasn't made him bitter against boxing, because he's a boxing historian, a boxing enthusiast and he has a wealth of knowledge about boxing. And he can share that knowledge.

I watched hundreds and hundreds – I used to get bored watching them. Mike used to come alive watching them, and I used to doze off. He was just passionate; he loved them, he loved watching black and white footage of the old fights. Unbelievable. He'd know all the details of them. Every fight. Every round. He'd analyse what they could have done differently. How it might have changed the history of the weight divisions if the guys that had lost had won instead.

To me, there's only so much boxing you can watch. To Mike, there wasn't enough.

ONE OF THE FINEST HUMAN BEINGS

In '85, we could see Cus was getting sick. He was still getting around the gym and everything, still very enthusiastic. It was hurting Mike, it was hurting Tom, it was hurting me, it was hurting everybody – because Cus d'Amato was a wonderful human being. That's the only way you could describe the man, as a wonderful human being. One of the finest human beings that God had put on the earth.

Cus didn't rule Mike with an iron fist – it was a father/son love. And I think for the first time in Mike's life he'd met somebody that he truly believed was genuine. He knew in his heart of hearts that Cus was genuine. Cus wasn't there to make financial gain out of Mike; Cus was there because he knew he could nurture the man to become the great champion that he became. And it was very, very sad, it was destroying.

When Cus died, God rest him, even though I was made to feel like family, I still felt at that moment in time that it wasn't my place to be there. The people that were there were the ones that should have been there from the beginning. I bowed out at that moment to let the mourning go on, for a time for Mike to spend with Cus. Then I went back.

When Cus died, I believe that's when the self-destruct button was pressed on Mike. That's what I believe.

FAMILY

Jay was there when I was there. He'd done a little bit of sparring with different fighters. He was helping Cus do the bandaging, he was helping doing the training and he was just one of the team that was there. Jay's a lovely guy and he's been Mike's close friend as well. He's in Las Vegas now, training a couple of fighters. But he was there to learn to be a trainer, whereas I was there and Mike was there to learn to be a fighter. So Jay was there getting Cus's guidance how to train fighters, I was there getting Cus's guidance on how to fight. And Jay was just one of the family.

You could say he's like Mike's stepbrother. That's what you could say was the link. And he was there for a lot of Mike's fights; he was in his corner, the same as Tom Patti was in his corner for a lot of Mike's fights. They were there from the beginning of Mike's career with Cus, and they were part of Cus's family as such. There was none of them blood linked except Camille and Marnie, but they were like adopted family. It was Cus and Camille and Marnie that brought these people together.

TRUMP TRIP

After Cus had died, Mike got this new Rolls-Royce – a limousine this time! We were up in the Catskills and Jay had to bring the car to New York City to get a phone fitted into it.

So Jay said, 'Do you want to drive down to New York City with me, Joe, to get the phone fitted?'

I said, 'Yeah! Of course I do!' Well, it's not every day of the week you get to drive in a Rolls-Royce limousine. 'Is Mike coming down?'

'No, Mike's not coming down. It's just me and you. We've got to drop some stuff off for Mike.'

'Yeah, no problem!'

So I'm in the front of the car with Jay and we're driving down. We drive through the Catskills and we drive down through the Bronx. Well, as far as I remember, we brought it down to a company called DD Collan Motors in Manhattan, and we had to drive down through the Bronx in the early hours of the morning. It's half-six, seven o'clock in the morning, and there's all these vans with tricolours on, all the Irish lads who were living in the Bronx going to work. So there's me leaning out of the front passenger-seat window of this Rolls-Royce limousine, shouting, 'Hey, Ireland! Ireland!' and all these Paddies driving their vans looking up.

I was only young, it was good fun. Little did they know that this was Mike Tyson's limousine, this is Mike Tyson's stepbrother driving the limousine and this is Mike Tyson's friend yelling from the passenger seat. If only they'd known.

Well, they'll know now if they read this, if any of them can remember this mad Paddy driving down through the Bronx in a Rolls-Royce limousine on the expressway in the early hours of the morning screaming out of the window.

We brought the car into this showroom to get the phone put in and we were introduced to the lady that owned the company. She had photographs in her office of all the celebrities that she'd supplied Rolls-Royces for – Frank Sinatra, Don King, James Brown – all these different stars, film stars, on the wall, and the next photograph was Mike Tyson's Rolls.

It was a lovely day that day. Wherever DD Collan Motors were, I can't remember, but we got the subway somewhere and they were going to give us a courtesy car. We said, no, no, we'll walk around the city. So we went off to Trump Tower, Donald Trump's apartment block in Manhattan. We went to Trump Tower because Robin, Mike's ex-wife, had an apartment there.

I was introduced to Robin and her mum, Ruth Roper. At the time, I think he was only courting her; I don't think she was his wife, it was just boyfriend-girlfriend at that stage. She was stunning, that's the only way you could put it. Just stunning. There was no camera magic or anything to make her look good; she just looked fantastic. Jay introduced me to her and her mum. This is Mike's friend Joe from Ireland, and we've brought the car down. We didn't really speak, just hello and that was that.

Then Jay did what he was asked to do for Mike and then we went off round the city and eventually collected the car – they'd done the work in the day – and went back up to the Catskills. It wasn't as exciting going back up as it was going coming down because there wasn't all the tricolours! But we got back up and Mike was so excited about his new toy in the car and it was just lovely.

Mike's generosity in wishing to give gifts to friends, even in the early days, was quite a thing. At that time, it was all 'shell suits' – Gloria was the make, Gloria New York. Mike gave me this black shell suit. They were a few hundred dollars each. It was nothing to Mike but it was an awful lot to me. I've still got it at home. And he gave me loads of things that he'd collected over the years.

HANGERS-ON

The hangers-on, those who told him they were his friends, the huge entourage that got wrapped around him later, that came with Don King. That was never Cus. Cus wouldn't have tolerated that. I didn't know the man for an awful long time but, for the short time that I knew him, I knew that he wouldn't have tolerated that. I know that in my heart of hearts. And Jim Jacobs and Bill Cayton – I met them, lovely men, dignified men – they wouldn't have wanted all that baggage. That was something that came with Don King, all these people jumping on the bandwagon with Mike. They're not true friends. I've seen it over the years. They were all hangers-on. They weren't there from the beginning.

The people that were there from the beginning are still there, that are alive. Tom Patti and Jay Bright, they're still there now. Mike is still best friends with Tom and best friends with Jay. So the chaps that are still there for him is where he's built up friendships. Tom Casino is still there, that's a very important part of Mike's boxing career and friendship. Now, there's a photographer; he's the No. 1 Showtime photographer, the No. 1 sports photographer in the world – he's a very humble man, but he's probably the greatest sports photographer ever. He's won the accolades of winning Sports Photographer of the Year, and he is a very, very close friend of Mike's. He's been up to the Catskills a number of times over the years; he's been friends with Cus and Camille, and he's been there more or less from the beginning. And he is still one of Mike's closest and trusted friends and I'm proud to say he's my friend as well. And Mike, Tom Patti and Jay Bright are my friends. I'm proud to call them my friends.

CHAPTER THREE

New York

SPARRING WITH THE ENEMY

After sparring with Mike, I got employment sparring with future opponents of Mike's. They employed me to spar with them because I had the recognition. I'm not saying a great reputation, I hadn't got such a great reputation, but I'd been introduced to different people as Mike's sparring partner that Mike hadn't put down.

They wanted to know if they could put me down because, if they were going to fight Mike in the future, they wanted that little bit of 'Well, we've knocked out the guy that Mike didn't knock out'. They wanted to do this, psychological, you know. So I was employed to spar with Alex Stewart, Mike's opponent. Alex was originally from London, but at that time he was based in America – Brooklyn, New York. He was being trained by a guy called Edwin Viroette. He was the 'prospect' – Alex 'The

Destroyer' Stewart, that was his nickname. He was knocking everybody out. He was up there, though, because he gave Holyfield nine good rounds and I think he got stopped on a bad cut against Holyfield.

Alex was a powerful puncher. He was fast – he just wasn't as fast as Mike. Mike unfortunately caught him early and knocked him out in the first round. Good fighter, Alex, very, very good fighter, but he got caught. But that's heavyweight boxing. Mike caught a lot of guys in the early rounds and knocked them out.

Then I was employed to spar with Carl 'The Truth' Williams before he fought Mike. I sparred with him in Gleason's gym in Brooklyn. Carl was a big tall heavyweight, rangy, lanky. I got in close. I had some good sparring with him. The same thing again. They weren't as fast as Mike. Mike stopped him in the first round (21 July 1989).

I loved the sparring. So many world champions. That's one thing – I was always recognised as a great sparring partner. And I was, because I had good hand speed, but I never had the knockout punch. I never had the big punch, so I wasn't too much of a risk for middleweights or light heavyweights. You know, if every heavyweight had concussive knockout punching, they wouldn't really be keen on sparring with a middleweight/light heavyweight. You couldn't get light heavyweights and middleweights to spar with Tyson because he was a concussive, heavyweight knockout puncher, but light heavyweights and middleweights would spar with me. I had the speed to move with them because I had fast hands. Cus used to say I had fast hands, God rest him. So I'd spar with middleweights, light heavyweights. I've sparred with a number of boxing champions all over the world.

It was during this period that I was working in The Lady Liberty Tavern because you couldn't make ends meet by sparring, so I had to do some different work. I was working on the building sites. At sparring, you got paid by the round, $50–$100, depending on who's who, their status. I sparred with a lot of fighters in Gleason's. I sparred with Iran Barkley and Chris Reed, who were light heavyweights. Iran Barkley, what a tough man he was.

Gleason's was run by Bruce Silverglade and Ira Becker. They ran a fantastic gym. As you walk up the stairs to go into Gleason's gym, there's a big load of writing above the door to fit any man that walks through these doors, to know that you have the potential. It's lovely, really fits the environment of a boxing gym:

'NOW, WHOEVER HAS COURAGE AND A STRONG AND COLLECTIVE SPIRIT IN HIS BREAST, LET HIM COME FORWARD, LACE ON THE GLOVES PUT UP HIS HANDS'
VIRGIL, 70–19 BC

It has three big sparring rings. Champions come from all over America and all over the world to spar. It's an open gym; you pay your subs, and different managers can use it. You've access to some of the best cutsmen in the world. There were different trainers there, and they would all try and help; even though you might be a future opponent for maybe one of their fighters, they would still have the time of day to help people. There was rivalry, great rivalry, but there was no animosity. Guys would help each other. There was a great atmosphere, and there is still to this day a great atmosphere in Gleason's gym. Gleason's gym, the home of champions – that's what they say about it. It's at 75 Front Street, on the Brooklyn Bridge. They pronounce it 'frawnt', not 'frunt'. It's on the Brooklyn side and it's a lovely, lovely gym. The atmosphere's great and I've watched some great champions there.

MY JUDAS PUNCH!

Then I got employed to spar with Mitchell 'Blood' Green, who went the distance with Mike. There's a bit of history between them – they had a bit of a spat once that became widely publicised without anyone really learning the truth. Mitch was managed at the time by Vincent St Angelo, who'd been involved with the Rocky Graziano era. I had some great sparring sessions with him. Carl Williams had never put me down and Mitch never put me down either.

He was a big man, Mitchell Green, 6ft 5in. Great fighter. I sparred with him at Gleason's. He was fast, but he hadn't got the power of Mike. He'd the speed, but not the power. Mike had the speed and the power. He and Mike had a great fight in May 1986. He lost but went the full 10 rounds. Tough man, Mitch Green. Street fighter.

Now I'd sparred Mitch for a long time, and I'd watched Mitch sparring. After the bell, Mitch would throw a couple of punches. The bell would go, the buzzer, so a lot of fighters drop their guard, and Mitch would land a punch after the bell. Not a knockout shot, but just a stinging shot, like 'I'm the daddy'. He wouldn't say that, but you know what he means, right.

I'd had to suffer it for days and days. And other fighters had to suffer it for just as long. So I thought to myself, 'Yeah, I'll sort you out!'

On this particular day, for whatever reason, I wasn't in the mood to be hit after the bell and to get 'I'm the daddy'. I'd been taking it for loads of sparring, and I hadn't retaliated. But just this particular day, whatever was going on in my mind, I wasn't – stuff it. So, anyway, the buzzer went, Mitch threw his usual after-the-bell double jab, real fast, then dropped *his* guard. This time, after he'd done his two shots, I gave him an unmerciful shot. Bam!

The bell had well gone. It was a proper liberty punch that I threw. Big right hand right into the eye. And I damaged his eye. I went back to the corner. I'd done two good rounds with him, two right good rounds. Anyway, I said that will do me today.

His eye had swollen up and he was going mad. 'Look at my eye! Look at my eye!' he's going.

So I stepped out of the ring because I thought to myself, 'He's a dangerous powerful man.' He'd been taking the same sort of liberty so many times and I thought I'd give back to him a taste of his own medicine. Then I started to pack up for the day.

So his trainer, Vince, is going mad. He's saying, 'No! He has got to go another round, minimum of three rounds!'

I said, 'No, I'm doing the two today.'

And my dad stood up on the ring apron and he said,

'My boy only wants to do two, that's all he's doing today. He's not a pro fighter, he's still an amateur, he's obliging you. All right, you've given him some money but he's obliging you, he's not contracted to you or anything like that. If he only wants to do two, he's only doing two.'

I said to my dad, 'Grand.'

So we went out to the back where the rows and rows of metal lockers were to get the gear off and clothes on and stuff.

Mitch Green came thundering through. Next of all, Bang! And again, Bang! And the row of lockers were shuddering! It felt like an earthquake. Bang! And he's screaming, 'Look at my eye! Look at my eye! Nobody does this to me! I'm Mitch Green! Look at my eye!'

I said to my dad, 'We'll just go home now, we'll leave early today right.'

And Mitch went on smashing the lockers because obviously he could see his face and his eye in the mirror now at this stage, and because it *was* a Judas punch.

But he'd been throwing two punches after every round had ended. And I was just tired of it, so I'd thought, 'Well I'll show him.' If he can do it, so can I. And he dropped his guard. And he wasn't looking.

I had no business throwing it, I had no business whatsoever throwing that punch, bang, straight into the eye. It was an open, sucker punch, whatever you want to call it; it was a free punch. Bang. It wasn't going to knock him. But it marked his eye, came up like a little bubble under his eye, and he ended up punching the locker, screaming and shouting.

I got showered, quick wash, and I left. Next day, I came into the gym, it was like nothing had happened, good as gold.

But you could see the little swelling under the eye.

LIBERTY AT THE LADY LIBERTY

At the time I was doing the door in a pub in New York on Wall Street, with an entrance on two streets – Pearl and Wall Street. It was called The Lady Liberty Tavern, not far from the World Trade Center. It was an Irish guy called Tim McMahon owned the pub. He was from Listowel in Kerry. He'd actually had seven pro fights unbeaten.

I was the maitre d'. I wasn't a bouncer or a doorman. I was there in a security capacity, but he had a pub that was done like a restaurant as well. He was an Irish man but ran the pub like an English pub. He had 10 lanes of dartboards.

The pub was the main seller of Watneys beer because Wall Street was very English orientated, with the relationship between Wall Street and the London Stock Exchange. So Tim was cashing in on the English side. He was selling roast beef, Yorkshire pudding and roast potatoes. As I say, I was the maitre d', and different sections would have different waiters. If there was a section that was full, and there was a section that was empty, you would usher people, you know, 'Table for two?' And you'd also be keeping an eye on them. Another section was the bar, and there was yet another section with a bit of music. It was a really nice place. My two friends in New York City, John Lawlor and John O'Shea, had come to the pub on the door. They were from Kerry like Tim – John Lawlor was from Listowel and John O'Shea was from Tralee.

We were living in Jersey City at the time, and my dad and my sister used to get the trains into the World Trade Center. On my first day there, my dad and sister were going to look at an apartment in Staten Island. As the pub was down close to the Staten Island Ferry, I said, 'Come in for a drink later, it's a lovely pub.'

They didn't take the apartment – it turned out that the guy wanted three months' rent and a month's rent security up front, which meant four months really, so it was too much. We ended up in one not far from Gleason's gym. Martin Snow, who was a boxer in Gleason's, a man mountain, powerful man, had put me in touch with Chuck, a friend of his, who got me an apartment down in Brooklyn, on 89th and 5th. We lived above a Greek guy called Tony Castanalonikas, who had a delicatessen – Tony's Deli. Fantastic, beautiful area, Bayridge, in Brooklyn.

Anyway, my dad and sister came to see me after seeing the apartment. I was talking to a chap, so I opened the door and said to them, 'Do you want to go on in?' They went in for a drink, and I said I'd see them shortly.

First, I just wanted to go down and check the toilets and make sure that there was nothing untoward going on. So I went in and there's a guy sniffing cocaine. So I said to him, 'You have to leave. We don't allow that.'

But he stayed sort of bent over, getting ready to do his cocaine.

I said, 'Hey, cut that out! You know we don't allow that. You'll have to leave.'

That's when he straightened up. Head and shoulders above me. 6ft 5in.

He says, 'Put me out.'

'Look, there's no call for that. I don't want any punch-ups.'

This guy was in a suit and he was obviously a stockbroker of some description. The last thing I want to be doing is getting into punch-ups down on the Wall Street district and get myself into serious trouble. I was doing my boxing.

So I said, 'Look there's no need for that. You're bang out of order, what you're doing is wrong; two wrongs don't make a right. Best you leave. Look, I won't walk out as if I'm putting you out. You walk out of your own accord, in case you think I'm going to try and embarrass you.'

'Right,' he said, 'I'll leave.'

I said, 'OK. I'll wait and you walk out, or if you want I'll walk out first.'

And he walked out first. But, by the time I walked out, he'd gone over to his friends. He was having his drink, not even making the effort to say goodbye to his friends or anything like that and I could see that he was pointing over at me. He was laughing. He had six or eight of his friends around him and they were laughing.

Now I don't mind people laughing *with* me, but I'm not going to have anybody laughing *at* me. So I went over.

'I've asked you to go; I've told you in the toilets that I wouldn't embarrass you. You're the one that's making a big issue, you should have just left. You're leaving now.'

Remember, this is the first day my dad and sister have come to the place, and I've told them it's a super friendly pub, never been a row, not when I'd been there. Now it looks like all hell's about to break loose!

I thought to myself, 'Well, he's gone. I don't care if the other six or eight take liberties with me, he's gone. I'm going to cave his face in.' You couldn't miss him, big, big man, square jaw, couldn't miss him. I thought to myself, 'He'll do for me.'

Bang! He was unconscious before he hit the ground. It was a cracking right hand.

Great shot. But it was the temper that did it, the frustration – after explaining to the man, I've been nice to him, then he's laughing at me.

But the rest of them, they weren't having it. So all hell *does* break loose.

The DJ, Joe, was a semi-professional jet skier, a fit guy from West Chester, Upstate New York. Lovely guy, martial arts expert. He jumps down off the DJ booth and he's fighting. My dad's in, he's having a row. My two friends, the two Kerry Johns, John O'Shea and John Lawlor, they're in too. So the odds aren't all against me because I've got my dad, the DJ and my two friends. Even my sister, fair play to her, jumps up! I don't realise this till I spin around and she's up on some guy's back! Some guy's gone to hit me from behind and she jumps on to his back and she's pulling. It was a proper brawl.

So, anyway, when it's all over, there's seven or eight of them have to be hospitalised. I was expecting the owner, Tim McMahon, to have a fit, but, being true to form, ex-fighter, ex-professional boxer, he said, 'You didn't start it, but you finished it, that's the most important thing!' And as long as none of his friends from Kerry were hurt! Genuine good guys.

They said to me, 'Look, Joe, you're going to get yourself into trouble having brawls in pubs.'

I said, 'It's the first time!'

LENNOX LEWIS

I boxed Lennox on 6 July 1985, Independence Day weekend in America, and it was a prestigious tournament up in Alexandria Bay, Upstate New York, on the Canadian border. It was the New York All Stars made up of the New York State Champions and the New York City Champions – the best of the best were going to fight the Canadian All Stars.

The star of the New York team was a welterweight called Frankie Liles who went on to shine bright and win the world professional super middleweight title.

The star of the Canadian team was Lennox Lewis and he also went on to shine bright. He won the world professional heavyweight title. At the time, Lennox was ranked No. 2 in the world super heavyweight behind Teofilo Stevenson, of Cuba. Lennox had got the bronze in the 1984 Olympics and he'd beaten Riddick Bowe to win the gold in the 1988 Olympics. In the 1984 Olympics, he lost to Tyrell Biggs, the American, and he got the bronze. Francesca Danielli, the Italian, beat the English kid, Bobby Wells, who beat me. Because the Cubans had boycotted the 1984 Olympics in Los Angeles, Teofilo

Stevenson was still the No. 1 amateur super heavyweight in the world, but Tyrell Biggs went pro, so Lennox held the No. 2 ranking.

A couple of weeks before the Alexandria Bay tournament in 1985, Lennox had fought in an international, Canada versus the USA, and he'd knocked out the American No. 1 super heavyweight. So the New York super heavyweight didn't want to fight him. Maybe, for some reason, he didn't feel he was good enough. So they didn't have a super heavyweight to fight with the Canadian team and they were struggling for somebody for Lennox.

I was boxing in New York at the time. I'd gone over with the Irish team and I'd stayed on with the acceptance of the Amateur Boxing Association in America. I was getting great treatment, getting treated with the utmost hospitality. I wasn't doing it for money. I was there on a holiday visa as such, but I was entitled to box amateur. I was sparring with Tyson at the time and, as far as I was concerned, I was holding my own against him. I wasn't being put down, I wasn't being smashed into the ground. So I thought, if I can take Mike Tyson's punches, I can take Lennox Lewis's punches. Sparring with Mike had given me great confidence. So I said, 'Look, I'll fight Lennox.' I was aware of who he was and I said, 'I'll fight him.'

And I got the opportunity. I won the New York State Golden Globes and I got the opportunity to fight on the New York All Stars team against the Canadian All Stars in the tournament at Alexandria Bay.

At the time, Lennox was weighing at least 16lb–20lb

heavier than me. I was only weighing in at heavyweight, amateur heavyweight. He was a lot bigger and heavier. And he was a fine athlete. He was fantastic, unbelievable.

I remember Lennox's speed. He had unbelievably fast hands. He didn't have that power that Mike had, but he had fast, fast hands. An unbelievable reach. He was so tall. And he was a gifted boxer. He had boxing off to a fine art. I know I was on the receiving end of his punches, but it was lovely to watch such a beautiful big man have so much class, so much ring skill, so much gift.

Without a shadow of a doubt, he had unbelievable ability. But all I had was 'I can fight'. I couldn't box to Lennox's ability; I couldn't stand there and box because he was taller, he had a longer reach and he was faster. So I had to get underneath his guard. So I had to get Lennox to fight *my* fight; I had to bring him into the trenches, had to fight in close. And it was a great fight. It was three three-minute rounds. And it went to points.

I believe in my heart of hearts that I won. I wasn't the star, far from the star. Lennox was the star, and they awarded him the fight. I didn't really agree with it, but I'm not at all bitter against Lennox for getting the decision because of what he went on to achieve. It was an honour to share the ring with him.

I can call Lennox my friend because we became friends and I got to do Sky television for the Lennox/Franz Botha fight in London. I was interviewed by Sky to help promote the fight, and told my experiences of Lennox. I've been a guest of Lennox's down at the Lennox Lewis Centre, and all that. I've played chess with Lennox. I joke that I've never beaten Lennox at chess either, but it was a lot less painful to lose at chess than it was in the boxing ring.

He's a thorough gentleman and a very private man. I've met his mum, Violet, and he has a wonderful relationship with her. I'm very close to my parents and it's wonderful to see Lennox, who at one time was the undisputed heavyweight champion of the world – the most powerful man on the planet at that moment in time – to be so gentle, so close, with his mum and to portray it on television; it's lovely to see.

You've got a savage sport – because boxing *is* a savage but disciplined sport – and you've got the heavyweight champion of the world, and so people, this Ban Boxing Brigade, try to portray it as savagery, so the heavyweight champion of the world has to be a savage. But you've got to see him, so gentle with his mum and not in any way shy of portraying that relationship.

And he has been a great ambassador for boxing.

THE LONELIEST PLACE IN THE WORLD

People say the boxing ring is the loneliest place in the world, but I can tell you a place that was lonelier for me than the boxing ring. I've been in the boxing ring over 100 times boxing, and I've been in the boxing ring thousands of times sparring. And it is lonely, but one time in my life was much lonelier.

I always liked to go home at Christmas because Christmastime with my family has always been important, and we've always been together. Since then, we've all got families and all gone our separate ways, as families do, but, until then, we were always together. I was in New York on my 21st birthday – 15 November – and, if I'd have gone home from New York for the 15th, it would have been very difficult to go home again at Christmas, to be able to afford to go home again at Christmas, and also with the immigration maybe questioning why you're going backwards and forwards so close together. So I sacrificed going home on my 21st birthday so I could be at home for Christmas.

At the time, I was working on a building site in New York, and there wasn't anybody that I could share my 21st birthday with. So, after work, I went out and had something to eat and just moped around and was feeling really sorry for myself.

I'd been away for my 18th birthday as well, but it wasn't as sad because I was in the company of friends and I could celebrate with them. But in New York at that particular time there wasn't anybody around me that I could tell. So I wanted to leave phoning home to very soon before I went to bed because I knew I was going to get emotional, and, as soon as the phone call was finished, I could just go to bed and sleep off the pain that I would have been going through. Because I knew what to expect, I knew the pain was going to come.

I was living in Brooklyn at the time, in Bayridge, at 89th Street and 5th Avenue. 8195 5th Avenue. I used to get the in-train back from New York City, Manhattan, into Brooklyn. When I came up out of the subway, it was near to midnight but it was like the early hours of the morning in Ireland, so my family were asleep. I'm standing on 86th Street and 4th Avenue and I rang home.

My dad answered the phone. 'Hello?' He was drowsy, awakening from his sleep. 'Hello, hello, who's that?'

'It's Joe.'

'Joe! Why didn't you ring?' I could hear him getting my brothers and sisters out of bed from their bedrooms. 'Get up! It's Joe on the phone! How are you? Are you all right?'

'Yeah, I'm all right, Dad.'

Next of all, my brothers and sisters are singing Happy Birthday to me over the phone. They're all in Dublin at the family home and I'm standing on 86th Street and 4th Avenue.

And the tears, oh floods of tears. I was surrounded by 10 million people and I was the loneliest man on the planet at that moment in time because I wasn't with my family on my 21st birthday. I've been lonely in the boxing ring, but there was nowhere at any other time in my life that I was as lonely as I was that moment in time, when my family were singing Happy Birthday to me over the phone, and I was standing in Bayridge in Brooklyn in New York City on my own.

TOENAIL

I was working on a building site in America and I was unloading the back of a lorry with a black guy called Oliver. And Oliver was handing me down what I thought was one sheet of plywood, but there was a second sheet. And the second sheet had dropped when I didn't have the grip of it, and it smashed through my boot and smashed my toes, the big toe taking the worse smack. The nail had burst off completely. It smashed my toes to bits. I've got a good pain tolerance, but the pain was so severe it was unbelievable. Oliver jumped down off the back of the wagon and a couple of the Irish guys I was working with, Tom Carroll and Francis Quinn, took me out the back. I had to hide because I was illegal, even though I was working under a genuine name; I hadn't got what's called the Blue Shield cover which is the insurance cover. If the shop steward had insisted I go to hospital because of the injuries, my cover would have been blown, so I couldn't risk going to hospital. So, when the shop steward had gone, Tom, Francis and Oliver cut the boot off my foot. My toe had burst right open, the toenail had burst off and the toe had gone to double its size. They put my foot underneath the cold water to try to take the swelling down. The cold water hit the open nail where the nail had gone. Pain shot through my body and I'd collapsed. I don't remember but the lads had held me up. I went unconscious. I'd been hit in the chin by heavyweight champions of the world and they didn't put me unconscious but this had knocked me out. Anyway, I'd been in the St John Ambulance Brigade years before, so I knew a bit about First Aid. I treated myself over a period of weeks. I patched the toe up and made sure that no infection had gone into it. And I really was very fortunate that an infection didn't get into the toe and eventually it got better. It's still not 100 per cent and my toenail has never grown properly as a result. But I wouldn't go to hospital because of the fear of the immigration.

Years later, when I was boxing professional in Belfast, I was trained by John Breen and Paul McCulloch. Paul McCulloch Sr was my trainer, and Paul McCulloch Junior is a boxer that I boxed with on many occasions in the Irish team. And the McCullochs are personal friends, they're just a lovely family, wonderful people. So I'm friends with Paul Junior, I'd been trained by Paul Senior, and I'm friends with the whole family.

So, while I was in Belfast, Paul was going down to visit his uncle Timmy who was living in Druncondra in Dublin. The family had raised money to buy Timmy an electric wheelchair because he'd lost his legs and they'd had his house fitted out to facilitate an electric wheelchair. They'd had a ramp and everything. The McCulloch family really pulled together to do everything for Timmy which was wonderful. So I was brought down to Dublin to meet Timmy. I wasn't going to talk about how he lost his legs; it's a personal issue. We're getting on great. It turned out that Timmy had worked for family of mine in Belfast years before, the Bannens. My dad's sister, Annette, is married to Dominic Bannen who was a doctor at the time. He's dead now, God rest him. But the Bannens were furniture people and Timmy had worked for them years before as a furniture restorer. So now we had a lot in common. The ice was well broken, and we're getting on great. And the subject came up about how he lost his legs. And he said that he'd had an ingrowing toenail that he neglected and gangrene had set into his leg as a result. They cut the leg off but they didn't get it in time to stop the spread of the gangrene to the other leg. So he ended up losing both legs as a result of an ingrowing toenail.

I felt sick to my stomach. He'd lost two legs as a result of neglecting an ingrowing toenail. I'd lost a toenail and smashed my foot to bits. I know it might be the realms of imagination but, if I hadn't had that St John Ambulance Brigade training and I hadn't looked after my foot with antiseptic and cleaning out the wound, I might have got an infection and ended up losing my legs.

I was very very lucky. Paul's uncle Timmy wasn't as lucky.

CHAPTER FOUR

Amateur Career

IRISH CHAMPION

I believe I was unfairly denied a place in the Irish Olympic team in two Olympics – '84 and '88. And both times for the same reason: some of the top boxing officials didn't like me. That was the reason I went professional in 1989 – after winning my fourth Irish title. I didn't want to go professional and I didn't do it because I thought, 'Well I'm going to get rich out of boxing.' I just loved boxing. I'd still be boxing amateur now because I just loved to box. I made good money away from the ring. I didn't drink or smoke and I'd no extravagant tastes. I just wanted to box.

I won my first senior title in 1984. I beat Cathal Ryan in the final.

In the final in 1985, I faced super heavyweight Bernie Deasy. He'd come over from Liverpool but he was originally from Castlebar. I lost a controversial decision.

In 1986, I'd gone down to heavyweight. I was beaten in

the semi-finals or the quarter-finals by a guy called Tony DeLoughry. He was a former middleweight and light heavyweight champion. He'd come up to heavyweight and was too fast, too experienced, and he beat me on points.

The following year, 1987, I beat him at heavyweight. I gave him a right good pasting. And in 1988 I won the senior title again at heavyweight.

In the previous five years, I'd been in one final, one quarter-final and won three titles at senior level. And I'd won two under-19s and a junior title before that.

In 1989, I worked my way to the final against Sean O'Regan. He was the hot prospect, the knockout puncher. He'd come from a very successful kick-boxing background. He was from Cork, from Rylane. His trainer's name was Dan Lane.

Sean was a martial arts karate expert, a kick-boxing champion. He was an Irish school teacher. He was a powerful man – 6ft 2in, solid, great physique on him – and he was unbeaten. Powerful, powerful puncher. And he'd been knocking everybody out. He was the new kid on the block.

I was the previous year's champion and I was on top of my game. But he was the new up-and-comer, the big puncher, so this fight had all the makings.

Tony Mahon and Benny Bracken were my two cornermen. They knew the heart that I had, they knew I had the heart of a lion. They knew that I had been hit by some of the best punchers in the world before, better punchers than Sean. They believed I could win. But, because of the rave reviews that Sean was getting, because he was knocking out a lot of guys, a lot of people I'm sure had doubts: 'Can Egan take this guy's punches?'

'Yeah!' Tony and Benny were saying. 'Keep your guard up!'

But I've always thrown caution to the wind and just got stuck in. Maybe not the best way to go about it when you're fighting a ferocious puncher, but I just got stuck in. There was no feeling out. It was straight in. Straight at each other. In the first round, in particular, he landed some right heavy blows.

I'm not saying his punches were having no effect on me, but they weren't stopping me in my tracks, where they'd been stopping everybody else.

When you're in the ring and the guy hits you with what is probably his best punch and you walk through it, it can be very demoralising for the guy that's punching. And I walked through some of Sean's best shots.

So I'm sure when he went back to his corner there had to be an element of doubt in his head. He'd been knocking a lot of people out, and I'm sure it was with the same or similar punches that he was hitting me with. A lot of the punches he was landing were hurting me. Head and body. But you've got to try and show no effect from the punches. If you start showing cringing and squealing, showing your face, it gives him a little bit of a boost. And you don't want to be giving him a boost. Some fighters try and smile, like, but sometimes that just shows that they've been given a great shock. So you try to show no emotion whatsoever. Even though they're hurting you, you just try not to show it.

I said a couple of things to him as well – 'Is that all you got?' – which sometimes you do, because I got warned a couple of times through the fight for talking. You do it because, first, you want to get them demoralised and, second, you want to try and anger them so that they throw caution to the wind and their style goes out the window and they leave themselves open.

I was pulling him in close, saying, 'My mother hits harder than you! Is that all you've got?' Things like that, niggling things, so that he'd drop his guard just for that split second so then I'd have a chance to land a couple of shots. And you do everything you can. But you're not actually cheating; it's just little things. Muhammad Ali was a master at winding his opponents up like that.

You want to win every round, especially in a three-round fight. I believed I was in front, but I still went out in round three as if I was behind. You still go for it as if you're behind.

My corner were very good. Tony Mahon was very experienced, he trained me more or less through my whole amateur career. He was saying, 'He's took your best shots! He's got nothing left! Go for him!' Just good pep talk.

It was a good fight and it was pretty close. But I liked to think I'd done enough to win. You go back to the corner, you're sort of half waiting – because I have had controversial decisions. Like the time I believed I'd beaten Bernie Deasy, but they gave the decision to him. So I thought, 'Well I hope they don't do this with Sean O'Regan', but they didn't, they gave me the decision.

Me and Sean embraced. We were after giving each other our best shots. I have the greatest of respect and friendship with Sean.

Shortly after, I got an invite down to box in Cork on Sean's bill, just before I went pro. Sean had come back from America after boxing with the Irish team and given a real good account of himself. Done Ireland proud and he'd had two good fights. Won one and lost one. The write-ups had been brilliant. So he came home to Cork as an Irish international heavyweight fighter and he had a great reception when he got home. So his trainer, Dan Lane, invited me down to box on his club show in Cork. They said they'd look after me with a lot of expenses. And I said, 'Great!' They flew me down from Dublin to Cork, which was great. And they looked after us, put us up in a fantastic hotel.

When I boxed Sean again, it was the same as when I fought him in the seniors, a great fight, very close. It was Sean's home club and he got the decision on points. But I didn't mind because I'd beaten him in the finals of the seniors, so I didn't mind losing to Sean in his hometown in his own club and it had been a close fight.

A very good fighter Sean was and he was a good guy after the fight. I'd beaten him in the national championships final, which was very important to me, and he'd beaten me in his club so it was very important to him.

THE MAN MONSTER

One of my amateur fights in London, I fought in the Porter Tun Rooms, at the Whitbread Brewery. We stayed in Canning Town next to Bruno's gym, in the Seaman's Mission there. They took us in to see Bruno.

It was a big charity evening. Terry Downes, the former

middleweight champion of the world, was doing the compering in the ring. Bruno was there, as was Richard Branson. It was a gentleman's dinner.

There was no weigh-in, so I never saw the guy I was fighting until the night. So I'm in the corner and I've seen what I can only describe as a man monster, with this massive hairy chest sticking out over the vest. I swear to God, he was a gorilla. He's coming to this side of the ring. My legs are doubly shaking because I've never fought a man with a hairy chest before.

I was showing confidence but, for the first time in the corner, I was terrified. Honest to God. My opponent was like one of them Italian porn stars. He was mad-looking.

My trainer said, 'Are you all right?'

The blood drained out of me.

He went, 'What's wrong?'

I said, 'Look at the hairy chest!' I couldn't believe it; I was terrified. He was a man. I was still a young teenager, a boy.

They were laughing. They said, 'All right, calm down, relax.'

When the bell went, I was so terrified that the first decent punch I threw, a desperation fear punch, knocked him out. I knocked him out in the first half a minute. But it was out of fear. I don't know where the strength came from, but as soon as they did the count it's over. Then, with the release of the tension, I jumped out of the ring.

'Bring on Bruno! I was a world beater. 'Anybody, bring them on!'

But I'd started to shake when I saw this guy come in with the hairy chest!

THE ATLANTIC CITY EXPRESS

In 1988, we were showboating the prospective American Olympic team. Normally, when the Irish team fight the Americans, we'd fight maybe the No. 3 and No. 4 American team because they have like 10 teams to choose from. The No. 1 team would fight the Cubans, the No. 2 team the Russians, the No. 3 team the East Germans, 4th and 5th, England and Ireland. But this was the No. 1 team. So I'm boxing the American No. 1 in Atlantic City, at the Sands Hotel. And I'm out the back in the changing rooms. I wasn't out watching the fights; I was warming up, getting bandaged up, so I didn't hear the introductions of any of the other fighters, or who they were fighting. Anyway, I do my walk to the ring, and I'm in the corner. Then Seldon's brought to the ring. He's walked in and it was like something you see on a world professional title fight. There was a big entourage walking in and he was being brought in like he was something very, very special. He was introduced as Bruce Seldon, 'The Atlantic City Express'! So, now I realise what all the big extravaganza is for: he's from Atlantic City! We're in Atlantic City! He's boxing for the national team and it's his hometown.

I went to my cornerman Mickey Hawkins. I said, 'This is at international level, it's not like a club-level fight, it's an international!'

And I'd never heard an international-level fighter being introduced with a nickname, which was a bit daunting as well. You've got your opponent facing you but then suddenly he's being introduced with a nickname that he's got in his hometown. So that sort of sends a bit of an extra tingle or shiver down your spine.

I said to Mickey, 'That's a bit unfair, he's introduced with a nickname!'

And Mickey said, 'Oh don't be worrying about his name, his name's not going to do you any harm!'

So I go out for the first round. And he was moving! He was a class act, a beautiful boxer, a beautiful fighter. And he was giving me a bit of a going over, a bit of a pasting.

For our fight, the referee was American. They had two Irish judges, an American judge and an American referee. For the next fight, there'd be two American judges, one Irish judge and an Irish referee, so they were alternating.

Anyway, I came back to the corner after round one, having taken a severe beating. It was a three-round amateur fight, three minutes per round. I'm saying to myself, 'I've got two more rounds of this! This guy's only warming up! He's out to give me a whipping! Is he ever going to slow down?'

As a fighter, your pride and your willpower and your determination are going to carry you through. But your cornermen, they're supposed to be level-headed because all fighters don't want to stop. All fighters, when they go on, want to hear the last bell. Win, lose or draw, you want to hear that last bell; you don't want to be stopped. It's a fighter's pride. And that's why you have cornermen there, they know what fighters go through, they know the pride that they carry, and they know that no fighter ever wants to stop. So they're there to say, 'Well, look, you've had enough now, you've got the heart of a lion, but we're thinking with our head, you're thinking with your heart, and it's time to stop.'

So I've come back to the corner and my two cornermen, Mickey Hawkins and Gerry Hannah, are saying, 'Right, you've had enough! He's punching lumps out of you. You've took a severe beating, you've done well to make it through the first round, we're going to throw the towel in.'

So I said, 'No! No way! I'm not retiring on this!' If the referee stops it, that's what he's there for. If a guy's taking too much punishment, the referee's going to stop it. But there was no way I was going to quit. And I said, 'No I'm not quitting on my stool!'

So I'm getting up for round two. Getting yourself off your stool knowing that it's just to get pounded to a pulp again is hard. To drag yourself off your stool when it's a 50–50 fight is hard enough, but to drag yourself up when it's a 95–5 fight because he's giving it to you hot and heavy, it was double hard.

The referee says, 'Right!' and I stand up from the stool and I'm looking across. And I could see in Seldon's eyes, and he's saying to himself, 'What's he coming out for round two for? I've just smashed him to bits and he's coming out for round two!'

So I've come to the centre of the ring, and he's looking at me, and I'm sure that's what he was thinking, 'I battered you, and you're coming out for round two! What are you doing?' And, for that split second that he was looking at me as the bell went, he didn't go into the attack. For that split second, he was a standing-still target, which I hadn't had for the first three minutes – the target had been moving and hitting me! So I hit him with the hardest body shot that I possibly could. He was standing still, but the referee had said box, the bell had gone, so it wasn't an illegal punch. As it landed, he went 'Oooohhhhh!' because, wherever I caught him, in the ribs, in the solar plexus, it took the wind out of his sails. And I could hear the pain in his voice. It was an unmerciful shot, a great body shot, right in, slugged it right in.

It wasn't a low punch, but it was enough to slow him down. That's all I wanted to do, slow him down so that I could land my punches, even if it was only punch for punch, because when I'd been getting punched I hadn't been able to land them in properly because he was moving so gracefully, so fast. He was a special fighter. I knew even as I was fighting him that he was going to go on to greatness.

Anyway, with that body shot, as I heard the pain in the groaning when it landed, it gave me a new lease of life because I knew then I could hurt him. The first round he was really bashing me, so when I came out for the second it was demoralising for him, and the fact that I'd landed this body shot was doubly demoralising for him, so he's really slowed down now.

So now I started taking over, because he's not moving on his toes now. He's now standing toe-to-toe and that suited me. My natural brute strength and sheer willpower was better at toe-to-toe; in the trenches, it was better for me, it suited me better. So, come the end of round two, I was starting to take over. Every punch I landed on him, I thought, 'This is payback for round one, because he'd given it to me in round one something shocking.'

At this stage, I'm oblivious to what's going on outside of the ring because I'm concentrating solely on the fight, but afterwards I was told the crowd were on their feet. It was a proper 'nobbins' fight, the crowd were standing cheering. The Americans in the crowd, because he was their local boy, The Atlantic City Express, had been cheering him. Now they were cheering a terrific fight between two great warriors. I went from taking a beating in the first round to dishing out a beating in the second. And I felt, 'I can win this fight! I've got the beating to this guy!'

When I had walked back to my corner at the end of round one, Mickey Hawkins and Gerry Hannah had been all doom and gloom, and you could see I was walking back to a demoralised corner, one that would throw the towel in. Now, suddenly, at the end of round two, they're alive, buzzing. They've got an *Irish* heavyweight that is going to beat an *American* heavyweight on his own turf in America. And not only in America, in his own city, which didn't happen very often. And *Irish-American* heavyweights have always been their pride and joy! They've had some of the best heavyweights in history. But it wasn't every day of the week that an Irish heavyweight beat an American heavyweight, in America.

Seldon was a great boxer, on that night I was a great fighter. And through the second round I didn't want it to stop.

You don't really feel the punches through the fight as such, the pain. It's very difficult to explain. Afterwards, when you're sitting down, and you're having a bowl of soup or something, then you start feeling the pain. During the fight, the adrenaline is pumping that much, and your sheer willpower to win keeps you going. And Irish fighters through history have been renowned for their resilience, their toughness. That's what we're known for, even though we might not be the most skilled fighters in the world.

But back to the fight. At this stage, it's even: he's won the first round, I've won the second round. But I was the one that was coming on.

It's funny, the first one-minute break between round one and two went so quick because I was going out to get pounded again. But the break between round two and three when I'm waiting to get out to go and give it to him seemed to drag on for ever! Like, when is this minute going to end? Now I'm buzzing to get back out!

At the start of the second round, the American referee had been watching me, as I came out, was I still OK to come out? Now, at the start of the third round, he was paying more attention to Seldon, was *he* OK to come out?

The third round. I was looking at him walking from his corner. Oh, it was great. The American referee was looking, because I was watching out of the corner of my eye. I had to win that last round because it was even Stevens – he'd won the first, I'd won the second.

They were talking in the corner: 'You've got the upper hand here! Press it home! Keep your foot on the pedal!

Stay on top of him! Go for it!' Motivational talk. Giving you that little bit of a gee-up. At that particular moment in time, wild horses couldn't have dragged me away from Seldon. I was going straight at him, straight at him.

We come to the centre of the ring. Touch gloves. Get stuck into each other again.

It was three minutes of punching, but I was landing three punches to his one. When the final bell went at the end, I was still standing in the centre of the ring punching. I knew in my heart and soul that I'd won. And his reaction was that his head sunk to his chest because he knew on that particular night he'd given his all and he'd lost to the better man on the night. And he went back to his corner and I was going crazy – that was my moment, and I knew. There was two Irish judges and one American judge, and there was no way on God's earth that the two Irish judges were going to vote against me – because I knew that I'd won two of the three rounds.

There were hugs, embraces, jubilation. Mickey Hawkins and Gerry Hannah were jumping for joy. And this is before the decision was announced. The crowd was ecstatic. Before the start of the fight, when Seldon was introduced, they were a very fair sporting crowd and they had given me a clap. But at the end of the fight you'd think they were all there for me.

The referee called us to the centre of the ring. He said, 'Put your hands together for an amazing fight! All of you, give a hand for two true fighters, two warriors!'

And the crowd gave us a standing ovation.

When he'd gone back to his corner, Bruce had looked

demoralised because he'd sussed, he had a fair idea that he'd lost. His cornermen had obviously said to him, 'You've just been in one hell of a fight, now be proud of yourself.'

Now he came out, a true sporting man. We embraced. And – you could see it in his eyes – he was unhappy for himself the fact that he'd lost, but he was happy for me that night!

Sometimes, when big men come in fighting, because they're getting close, because they're big men, there can be clashes of heads. But in this fight there wasn't. It was a clean fight. I had the utmost respect for him, he's a clean fighter.

And when we came to the centre of the ring, we embraced again and you could see in his eyes the respect and admiration, and at this stage friendship. You know the fight's over, we'd given each other hell and he knew it was my moment.

The referee acknowledged us again. 'A great fight!' Then he said it was a majority decision Ireland or whatever corner, I can't remember. It was unbelievable. Even though I knew I'd won, until I had my hand raised, I wasn't sure.

Anyway, I looked around, and there were 10 champions that we'd been introduced to that day: Jake La Motta, Rocky Graziano, Joe Frazier, Jersey Joe Walcott, Sandy Sadler, Alexis Arguello. Vito Antofermo, Billy Conn, Floyd Patterson, Chico Vejar. These former champions and former greats were all giving a standing ovation! I'd had standing ovations before, but I'd never had 10 champions of the world standing. There's no feeling like it in the world. You can't put it into words.

The fight helped Seldon too. He showed a lot of heart that night, he showed great heart. He was the national champion of America and he was being groomed for the Olympics, to be the next big thing. And he did go on to be the next big thing. As a professional, he won the WBA heavyweight title, in April 1995. He achieved what every fighter dreams about. Every fighter dreams of being world champion – ask any fighter who turns professional, any fighter that puts on a pair of boxing gloves as an amateur. Every fighter, whether they be flyweight or heavyweight, they dream about being world champion. Some get to live the dream, they get to be world champion, but there's millions don't. I was one of the ones that didn't, but Seldon went on to live the dream and became heavyweight champion of the world. And I envy him for what he achieved and I take my hat off to all he's achieved.

But that night was my night of nights in '88.

My dad, my younger brother Connolly and my younger sister Maureen were living in New York City at that time and had come up to see the fight. After the fight, I had to look all around for them – because we were getting cheers from the four sides of the ring. I was looking for my family. I was looking at the stage at the champions.

People joked, 'Oh he's milking the applause.'

I *was* milking the applause! I was loving it! I was a showman, always been a showman. Eamon Andrews, who did *This Is Your Life*, his brother Noel Andrews commentated one of the fights and he said, 'Joe Egan, you're the Abominable Showman!'

When you win a fight like that, you're entitled to the applause.

Bruce Seldon, being the sportsman and dignified man that he is, left the ring and let me have my moment. And I took it!

I saw my dad at that stage, I had eye contact with him and he was buzzing. I was looking at my sister who was buzzing too. And the Irish team that I could see that had come out to watch the fight were jumping for joy, different team members. Then there was the champions on the stage, they were giving me applause. And it was wonderful, there's no way to put it into words the feeling. I was loving it. For that moment, in my mind, I was the heavyweight champion of the world. I can put no other feeling to it other than winning the heavyweight title. It was just unbelievable.

When I walked from the ring, there was people patting me and grabbing me and hugging me. It was fantastic. So then it took me about 10 or 15 minutes to get back to the changing room.

RAGING BULL

When I got back to the changing room, the cornermen were very concerned because I was well bruised up and my face had been badly damaged. They were saying, Calm down, relax, let's get the doctor to examine you.'

I took my headgear off so he could see my whole face and the swellings. Whatever the doctors look for, whatever the telltale signs are for different injuries, they know what they're looking for. Now this doctor said, 'You've got some bad swellings. I'm insisting that you go to the hospital for an MRI scan, for a brain scan.'

So it put a little bit of a dampener on the win because I had to go to the hospital now. So, when you sit down, the worry is now that you might be seriously damaged. I'd had brain scans before. Normally, you get them done before fights to check that you're OK. I'd never had one done after a fight.

I'm sort of saying to myself, 'Now you realise what you've gone through, and you realise that these are the injuries that you've sustained.' A lot of swelling is a bit worrying. I was concerned. I was saying to myself, 'Think positive, hopefully it's just a bit of swelling, hopefully there's been no permanent damage, hopefully you're OK.'

So, anyway, they've got the ambulance ready to take me to the hospital because any time there's a fight there has to be an ambulance, medical people, paramedics, doctors, they're all there. The best medical care in the world is at any fight. Whether it be a small hall show or a Las Vegas show, they're strict on the medical. So the Irish officials were saying they'd come to the hospital with me. And I said, 'No, no, let one of the American officials come to the hospital with me. Please enjoy the hospitality of Atlantic City, they live this every day of the week, the Americans. Let one of the American officials come to the hospital with me.'

So I'm in the back of the ambulance with one of the American officials, the doctor and the ambulance crew, and the adrenaline is starting to wear off at this stage and suddenly the pain is setting in. And I'm sitting there and I'm feeling sorry for myself now.

The American official and the doctor were talking to each other. And I'm sitting there. And it's going through your mind what you've gone through, what injuries have you got. And you're feeling sorry for yourself because the pain is setting in now, you're feeling all the lumps and bumps. Even though I've won, I'm in a bad way.

Then I began wondering what we were waiting for.

It turned out they wanted to bring Jake La Motta, the Raging Bull, to the ambulance!

What I found out afterwards was that, all through my fight with Seldon, Jake La Motta had been standing on the stage fighting the fight with me – it was like a throwback to when he was fighting, in his glory days – it was a proper war – and, while he was doing it, he'd tripped, and he'd hurt his arm and cut his eye when he fell over.

So I'm in the back of the ambulance with the American official, a guy called Joe Gaffney, and he's saying, 'Are you OK?' I'm sitting there miserable, far too sore to speak, concentrating on the pain. I just nod.

Finally, Jake La Motta, the Raging Bull, is brought into the back of the ambulance. I'm sitting there and I look at him, because we'd met him that day.

And he looks at me and he goes, 'The Heavyweight. Great fight, kid!'

If you can picture it. I've got the Raging Bull telling me that I was in a great fight and he really appreciated it; *he* had enjoyed my fight. Well, there's no words to describe it. It was the best anaesthetic I've ever had in my life. In that split second, all my pain had just gone.

I went to the hospital with Jake, where we were both treated. I had the brain scan, the examination, and there was no serious damage done other than bad bruising and swelling. And my face was pretty swollen up but I was OK.

What I also found out afterwards was that, when Jake fell over at the ringside, my brother Connolly, who was only 15 at the time, went to take a photograph of him lying down on the deck, and the minder, the bodyguard said, 'Get back, kid! Get back, show some respect. It's the Raging Bull on the deck. The man never hit the deck in his fighting career!'

I DON'T UNDERSTAND IT!

After the fight, as far as I was aware, my dad, my sister and my younger brother were heading back to New York and I was going to see them a few days later. What I didn't realise was that, with the atmosphere and the excitement of me winning, my dad decided to stay on in Atlantic City. My sister Maureen had gone back to New York but my dad and brother Connolly stayed with me because they were concerned that I was OK and they wanted to enjoy the celebrations, the Irish team winning and me beating the heavyweight champion.

The Sands Hotel was magnificent. We had these suites in the hotel, there were two king-size beds in the suite and a separate room. I was sharing a room with Gerry

Hannah, who as well as being my cornerman was also one of the team coaches.

Anyway, when I got back to the hotel from the hospital in the early hours of the morning, I met some of the team in the lobby and they told me that my dad and my brother had actually stayed.

And I said, 'Oh right.'

They said, 'Your dad has got drunk.' And they said they had no alternative but to carry him to the room. He'd collapsed with the drink.

'Oh my God,' I said. 'What happened?'

'Well, he was playing the machines.'

When you're playing the machines in Atlantic City, the drinks are free. So he'd got my sister to get $50 worth of quarters and, as he was playing the machines, he called the waitress for a drink. He paid the girl with the money from the bottom of the machine and the waitress said, 'Oh no, the drinks are free while you're playing the machines.'

He said, 'Well, don't be going far, I'll need you again.'

So, by the end of the night he was paralytic, he was twisted. The atmosphere and the excitement of me winning and the drink had all taken its toll and he had to be carried to the suite. Gerry had said that my dad and brother could stay. The Irish team had carried him to the suite, and they'd put him in one double bed with my brother.

When I got to the room, I climbed into the other bed beside Gerry Hannah. Soon everyone's sleeping like logs, except me, because of the pain.

So the next morning I look in on my dad.

He suddenly sits up in the bed. His hair is like Don King's. 'I don't understand it!'

'Don't understand what?'

'I lost $50 in coins playing the machines, but I must have had $500 worth of drink! How do they do it?'

'Do what?'

'Imagine it! If Donald Trump was to open in Ireland. Play this machine with 50 pounds' worth of 10ps and drink all you like. Fifty Paddies drinking for nothing? Donald Trump would be broke in a month!'

HERO TO ZERO

We were supposed to leave Atlantic City the next day to go to New York, but instead they asked us to stay on to march in the St Patrick's Day parade because we'd just beaten the Americans. It was unbelievable.

So the word's gone round America now that I've beaten Seldon, I've beaten the No. 1. Four days later, the Irish team that had just beaten the No. 1 American team is fighting in New York, where the biggest Irish community in America is. There's all the excitement in New York. Because I'd lived in New York and I'd sparred in New York, I had a great following there anyway. And they were saying about me fighting again in New York four days later. Now I'd just been through what you can only describe as a war. But I was still on a high. And I'd just beaten the No. 1 in America. So, whoever the next guy they wanted me matched with in New York was, as far as I was concerned, it was bring him on.

I shouldn't have really boxed because my face was still badly swollen. But, true to Irish form, I want to fight. I want the glory again in New York that I had in Atlantic City. And I believed in my heart and soul that I could beat this guy, no problem, in New York, because I'd just beaten the No. 1.

What I didn't realise was that, because of the swelling, my skin had gone soft. I'd been badly damaged in the Seldon fight and, four days later, my skin had become very tender. So, the first decent punch I took in the first round in New York, my skin was split wide open – through the headgear and everything – and the fight was stopped.

My opponent was a good fighter but he wasn't in Seldon's class at all.

I had to go to hospital and get stitched up. So I didn't go back to the team hotel afterwards. I felt pretty demoralised at this stage because I'd gone from being the top to suddenly losing to a guy that on my night I believe I could have beaten – although I wouldn't describe him or any fighter as second-rate, every fighter's first-rate as far as I'm concerned.

I was working in New York at the time, but couldn't go to work with the stitches all in my face, so I thought I'd have a few days off. So I went to Philadelphia for a few days to visit a friend of mine, Paul Fitzgerald, who'd boxed on the Irish team with us. He was the Irish featherweight champion, and he was living in Upper Darby, Philadelphia. So I spent a nice four or five days with Paul and his family up in Philadelphia, where I had the stitches taken out, and it cheered me up to be with my friends.

CHAPTER FIVE

Heroes and Villains

EVICTION

In the early 80s, we used to sell logs and, first of all, we started selling sticks, bundles of sticks. We used to buy a bag of logs for £1.50, chop the log into a bundle of sticks, get the inner tube of a car, cut it across to make a big elastic band, put this big elastic band around a bundle of sticks and you could sell the bundles of sticks for 25p a bundle. So from a £1.50 bag of logs we used to make £7.50 for chopping them into sticks. And then we went on from selling the bundles of sticks to selling bags of logs. And then we used to go to my nan's yard and get 10 tonnes of logs delivered. And we used to chop the logs and fill our own bags. So we were doing really well. And then we used to put some of the bags of logs up into the backyard of our house. But somebody reported to the council that we were using the backyard of our council house as a business. In fact, we weren't selling logs from our house, we were selling logs from my nan's house, from *her* yard. She owned her own house. So they put the rent up on our council house, backdated it two years and said we owed them £6,000 in arrears. Young boys, chopping sticks! It was rubbish. So my dad fought them in court and he was winning and doing really well. Then an eviction notice was sent to my family but to the wrong address, presumably so that my family wouldn't get the notice and that the bailiffs would arrive unawares. But the postman recognised the name, realised it had the wrong address and delivered the letter to my dad, so my dad was aware of what was happening. And the bailiffs came and there was a stand-off battle. I was away boxing in Denmark for my country. Anyway, it was four days of pitched battles with different teams of bailiffs trying to get in, and a number of family friends in the house. But, in the battle that was going on, my mum took a bad panic attack and she cut her wrists, tried to kill herself. It was a bad, bad scene.

But I wasn't aware of any of this. I phoned home after I'd boxed and won my fight, to give my family the news and I couldn't get an answer. I was ringing and ringing and ringing, but couldn't get an answer. So I phoned my grandmother, my mum's mum, to find out what's wrong, how come I can't get an answer in my house. My nan, she's dead now, God rest her, answered the phone and she was crying.

I said, 'What's wrong? Well, what's going on?'

'Your mum's in hospital.'

'What?'

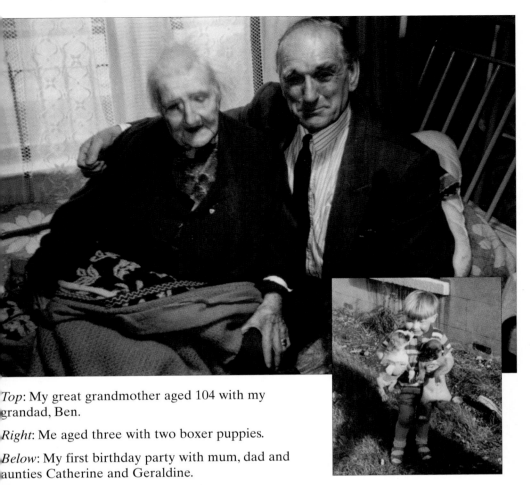

Top: My great grandmother aged 104 with my grandad, Ben.

Right: Me aged three with two boxer puppies.

Below: My first birthday party with mum, dad and aunties Catherine and Geraldine.

Right: After one of my first amateur fights with my trainer, Keith Drewitt (*right*).

Below: The Donore Boxing Club. I'm back row far right.

Bottom left: I've been boxing since the age of ten, winning four senior titles, two under nineteen titles and one junior title. This is one of my seven titles.

Bottom right: Signing Pro for Barney Eastwood.

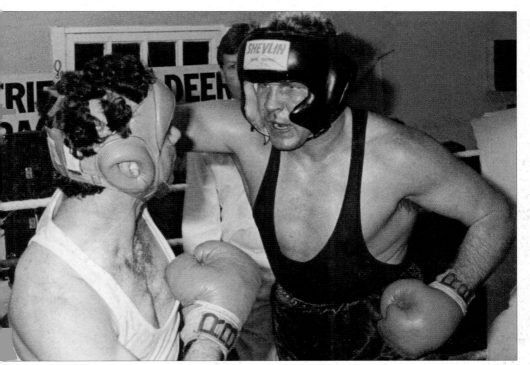

Top: I lost this close-fought battle after beating the same fellow, Sean O'Regan, in the Irish Championships.

Above and right: I used to love going to the gym, punching the bags and pads, and sparring. My nephew Tom would come and do the corner during sparring breaks.

Above: Proud Irish team captain at the Acropolis Games, 1987. Paul Thompson (*left*) and Sean Horkan, Team Manager (*far left*).

Below: Boxing Georgios Stefanopoulos at the Acropolis Games.

Left: The triumphant Irish team before fighting the Americans.

Middle left: Trading punches with Bruce Seldon 'The Atlantic City Express'.

Middle Right: Slipping under one of Bruce's punches.

Bottom: Bruce and I after the fight. "We'd given each other hell".

Three of Cus D'Amoto's World Champions. Floyd Patterson (*above*), Mike Tyson (*left*) and José Torres (*below*).

Top: The Egan Clan. (*Left to right*) my brother Emmet, sister Maureen, mum and dad, sister Constance (front), nephew Tom and sister Sinéad.

Middle left: Nephews Pearce and Daryl with my sister Ann.

Middle right: Mum with my brothers, Emmet and Connolly.

Bottom left: Dad, Maureen and I in Atlantic City before the Bruce Seldon fight.

Bottom right: Me, my brother Connolly and my friend Dennis Foynes on the subway in New York.

Above: "Great fight, kid". Inspiring words from one of the world's greatest fighters, Jake LaMotta, 'The Raging Bull'.

Above: My idol, Muhamed Ali, after the Mike Tyson/Kevin McBride fight.

'Your mum's tried to kill herself!'

I was shocked. My mum's tried to kill herself? My mum's the happiest person in the world! She's not dead! She survived?

And she started telling me about the eviction and she was crying, but it was hard to understand her, because, of course, she was just so devastated over her daughter.

I came home with the Irish team and I was picked up at Dublin Airport. Normally you get dropped off at your front door, but I got dropped at the bottom of my road because the man that picked us up was aware of what had happened and what had been going on because it was all over the news and he didn't want to drop me at my front door. He was upset over what was going on, as everybody that was genuine was upset. So I had to walk from the bottom of my road, which is only like 400 yards. I'm hurrying to my house. It was a sort of jogging run because I had my suitcases so it was hard to sort of sprint, a little bit of a jog, and I could see in the distance loads of my family's furniture out on the street. The bailiffs had finally got in.

The bailiffs hadn't been able to get in on their own, so the police had come, and my dad and the men that were in the house fighting off the bailiffs walked out because you can't beat the police and it wasn't the police's argument. There was a picture in the papers of my dad walking out shaking hands with the sergeant because the police didn't want to be doing this. It was wrong what was being done, and anybody that was decent could see that it was wrong what was being done.

By the time I got to my house, all my belongings and

stuff, all my family's belongings, were out on the street. My brothers and sisters had gone to family friends, and my dad was outside sitting on the rocking chair. He was making a stand for what he believed was right.

The Corporation were wrong in what they'd done, and they knew they were wrong in what they'd done.

But that was the eviction. My mum survived, but it's been traumatic for her ever since. It can break a lot of families and it did put a big strain on us all. Everybody suffered one way or another. We had an awful lot of support from the community at Ringsend, genuine people came to our support.

THE GREAT BACK DOOR FIDDLE

The first nightclub where I ever did the doors was Jules Nightclub on Baggot Street. It was formerly the Zhivago's Nightclub as in *Dr Zhivago*. 'Where love stories begin!' was the big motto. Pat Gibbons owned the nightclub and he was a friend of my amateur trainer, Tony Mahon. I was on the door there with Declan Foley, Johnny Nugent and Johnny Macintyre.

After that, I went to 30 different clubs. As your reputation grew, the clubs would offer you more money to try to poach you off other doors to work on their door. So you went where the money was.

Anyway, one time when I came back from America – because I was backwards and forwards to America over the years – I was with this particular club. It was a rave club. I'd been away in America for a good while and I knew nothing about this rave scene which seemed to have come about while I was away. Before I went away, it was like a disco scene. The drugs I'd had to deal with before in my clubs were on the streets. Now with the rave scene the drugs were *in* the club, and the drug was ecstasy. People were using it to dance, to fuel their energy for dancing. This particular venue was packed, really like sardines, and the owners used to keep it open till four, half-four, five o'clock in the morning.

But the place up the road, the Olympic, used to close at two o'clock. So there used to be crowds coming down from that nightclub to our club at half-two.

The cash desks on the sides would close at half-one, quarter to two, and the manager, the owner's brother and his family would be all around to make sure that you didn't let any more in – although you could let in a couple of people.

When I first came on the job, I said to my brother, who was the head doorman, 'What's the fiddle?'

There has to be a fiddle on most doors because the wages weren't great for the hours that you put in and for the risks that you took. So a bit of a fiddle, once they've closed their cash, was nothing to them anyway. You weren't taking anything out of the owner's pockets because they'd closed their cash anyway. The way I looked at it was, if there was some extra people in, they would be spending money over the bars so you're making money for them!

My brother said, 'There's no fiddle.'

'There has to be a bit of a fiddle.'

'No, no. They've got it tight. You'll never get anybody in. One or two, you could ask the manager.'

Anyway, he'd a team of doormen, all his friends and all my friends – Dave Mitchell, Michael Watson, John Murray, Mickey Burke, Noel Paget, Dave Cowley. Great guys, all ex-boxers, tough fellas. So it was a rock-solid team of doormen. It didn't matter how many went into the club, because they could handle it.

And this club used to pack them in. It was £10 in on a Saturday night and £10 on a Friday night, and there'd be 1,500 people maybe on three floors, so they were taking some money.

I said, 'There *has* to be a fiddle!'

'No.'

'What about the back door? They're not watching the back door?'

'The owner's brother on the back door.'

'Right I'll go and have a chat with him, sort something out.'

So I walked over on this particular night and got chatting to the owner's brother. And we're just talking, where he's living, and he said he's living at Castle Knock, which is a really nice part of Dublin, a very exclusive part of Dublin. So I thought he's obviously very well-to-do.

So I said to him, 'You're living in that part of Dublin, you've obviously done well for yourself with the club.'

'No,' he said. 'It's my brother, it's his club. I like to come in and help him. I don't do it for any money.'

'He doesn't give you any money?'

'No, no, he gives me my taxi fare home because I don't drive because we have a drink afterwards, so I don't like to be drinking and driving. They all stop back for a drink.

If it's a nice morning, I don't bother getting a taxi. I walk home and just pocket the money that John gives me for the taxi. If it's raining, I get a taxi home.'

I thought to myself, 'A hungry, greedy man like you.'

'Listen,' I said, 'if I was to give you £25 to just let a couple of my friends in through the back door, would you mind?'

He said his brother had been giving him £15 for a taxi home. Now he's been offered £25 and his eyes lit up like he's won this Las Vegas jackpot, the lottery's come in! He said, 'You'll give me £25 to let a couple of your friends in?'

'Yes.'

'OK.'

'Look, they'll pay for themselves because they'll spend money over the bar. I've said it to the club manager, but he doesn't want to know. If we let in a few extra people, they'll spend, makes it £50–£100, it's to the club's benefit.' Trying to make it sound saintly, but really he was interested in the £25.

So I went back round to my brother. 'Right, we've got him! He's bit! We might only get one hit, so let's go for it, get as many in as we can!'

So there were loads coming down from the Olympic, about 60–70 people – 'Can we come in? How much is it?'

'Cash is closed. Normally a tenner, five pound. Oh you've only got four quid? That'll do.'

So we had them all lined up between the front door and the back door. The back door was being used as the front door, if you can imagine it. And the double doors along Westmoreland Street, which was the emergency exit as you come in, went down to the basement, and you come back up in the club to ground level, then you went up to the top floor. There were three levels of this nightclub. Anyway, at the first hit we had about 70 people. They've given a fiver each on average and we had them all in, had five or six of the doormen outside keeping the line.

I'd arranged to do the knock and for him to open the door. So, when he opened the door we bundled them in, piled them in, as many as we could. It was like a stampede. When you've got like 1,500 people, maybe more, in a venue, an extra 60 or 70 isn't going to make a difference. But that extra 60 or 70 fivers shared out between six or eight doormen makes a big difference. So anyway he was like, 'You only said...' so I slipped him an extra fiver and I gave him £30. He was well chuffed.

This went on for about six or eight weeks gradually increasing the numbers every week. I think at one stage we probably had 200 people getting in the back door. I had a coat with eight pockets in it, like a duffle coat, and it was weighed down with money.

Anyway, this particular night there was a bit of a row at the front door. At the time, there were very few rows in the club because people were taking these ecstasy tablets which was the love drug, so everybody was loved up, and no one wanted to fight. So it was great, it wasn't a violent aggressive mood that they got with this particular drug, they just wanted to dance, so it was peaceful – great for a doorman!

Then these lads come along this particular night and they wanted into the club and the lads stopped them on the door. So a bit of a row started.

Now I'm weighed down with money. It was like lead weights. Anyway, the lads on the door were well able to handle the row, and there was a bit of punching going on. But I've seen this guy come up from behind one of my friends. He was going to do a sly move, so he could get a punch at my friend. As I threw my right hand, the manager was looking. I had pockets full of money. My jacket was swinging!

Anyway, after my punch landed, he hit the deck. I stood back against the wall, but there was nothing said.

After about six or eight weeks of doing the fiddle on the back door, the owner came up to me. Now I wasn't the head doorman – my brother was – but I was the biggest and I didn't mean to sort of take over running the show but my brother was a little bit inexperienced at night-clubs! I had a lot more experience because I'd started so young and I knew that we had to do a little bit of a fiddle after the till shut. And, as I say, it wasn't like the owners were losing, because they'd closed their cash anyway. So it's not like you're a robber. Anyway, I sort of took over organising the lads or whatever.

I said, 'What's the problem?'

He said, 'I believe there's somebody's on the fiddle.'

'Well, none of the lads here. The doormen are two of my brothers, Connolly and Emmet, and some of my closest friends, Dave Mitchell and Michael Watson, John Murray. It wouldn't be any of them.'

'No, worst thing... I think it's my own brother.'

'What makes you say that?'

'Well,' he said, 'he's starting to get a taxi home every night, which is a bit strange.'

I said, acting a bit stupid, 'What do you mean?'

'I give him his taxi fare because, when he comes in, he stays and has a drink, and he doesn't drive. And he usually stays on summer mornings. But I notice these summer mornings he's sort of roaming round the town.'

'Does he get a taxi home now?'

'All the time, which makes me a bit suspicious that he's fiddling extra money.'

I thought to myself, 'These are well-to-do people, how greedy can you get?' Every pound's a prisoner to these people. And you look and you say to yourself, 'Jesus. Ordinary people, working-class people, aren't so greedy. These are rich people, well-to-do, and so greedy.'

And he said, 'I'd like you to stand up at the back door and watch him.'

I thought to myself, 'Happy days!' Because before, if I'd stood up at the back door for any length of time, the owner, or the club manager, would have sussed out. 'What are you doing up at the back door?' So I used to have to walk by, because at that stage I was inside doing the opening of the door myself whereas before I was just doing the knocking. So when I was inside I had to be discreet. But now he's told me to stand up at the back door to keep an eye on his brother!

So I said, 'OK, but listen, it's best if you and the manager don't come up near the back door because then he might cop on that we're watching him.'

He said, 'OK.'

So I went up to his brother. I said, 'Listen, the owner, your brother, has asked me to come up and to keep an eye on you on the back door because the club has got so busy now that he's a bit worried about the crowds coming in and your safety, so it's best to put a security man with you, because he's concerned for your safety.'

'Oh,' he said, 'that's very, very good of him.'

I didn't want to let him know that his brother had told me to watch him because he thought he was fiddling him, so I said, 'That's what brothers are for.'

He said, 'Oh that's great!'

I thought, 'Now this is brilliant.' I'm up on the back door. I've got the owner and my manager told to stay clear of the back door!

It was a licence to print money. I was operating the door and then my brother would bring them in. Rather than having to bring them in a big crowd, you would bring them round in fours and fives and eights and tens. We were making a fortune on top of our door wages!

So, anyway, this went on for about four or five weeks. Then I said to the owner's brother, 'Listen, you're getting a taxi home regular every night?'

'Oh yeah,' he said, 'the extra £30 comes in handy. I just get a taxi home now rather than walk.'

'Listen, you might bring a bit of unnecessary attention to yourself, getting a taxi home regular. Your brother might think that's a bit suspicious.'

'You're right.'

'Listen, just walk from the club. Walk a half a mile away from the club and get a taxi. He won't see and it doesn't bring any unnecessary attention to yourself.'

'Good thinking!' he says.

So he started doing that.

After five or six weeks, the owner came up to me. 'Well done! He's said he's starting to walk home again. He must have copped on to you, Joe, watching him do the fiddle.' And he give me £50 for myself.

'Well done,' he said. 'But still float around up there in case he goes back to his old ways.'

PADDY FINN, MY HERO

When I started boxing, when I was a young amateur, I was with the Donore Boxing Club, and there was a heavyweight in the club who's since become a very, very close friend – Paddy Finn. He's one of the reasons I came over to Birmingham. He gave me the opportunity to start another life after my career had finished first time round and his career had finished. He had to have operations on his spine, which had ended his career.

We did a boxing night with different champions. There was Ritchie Woodhall and Rob Norton, Bunny Johnson, former British and world champions, all different champions. The radio station was there, and they were all being interviewed. Who did they want to emulate when they started out boxing, who was their hero, who did they want to be. Some of them were saying they wanted to be Muhammad Ali and he was their hero. Some were saying they wanted to emulate Marvin Hagler, and others were saying they wanted to emulate Rocky Marciano or Jake La Motta.

When it came to my turn to be interviewed and they asked who I wanted to emulate, I said, 'Paddy Finn', because at the time when I joined the Donore Boxing Club he was the Irish champion, and Ireland at the time was my world. So to be the Irish champion was like being the world champion.

I remember Paddy looking at me and he couldn't believe it.

I said it was true, it was sincere, that's what I wanted to be. I wanted to be the Irish champion.

I said this on the stage in front of former world champions, former European champions, former Commonwealth champions, and they were all taken aback because each of them had mentioned heavyweight and middleweight champions of the world. But I wanted to emulate Paddy Finn because he was the national senior champion of Ireland. He's a big man, he's 6ft 5in. And we all looked up to him, but not just because he's 6ft 5in, he's big in stature as well, he's a big presence. I wanted to emulate him, and he boxed at the same amateur club as me.

And I did achieve what Paddy Finn achieved; I got my name on to the same cup that Paddy Finn had his name on.

BOXING VERSUS CAREER

I'd won my fourth senior title. I'd come home from America to win the title. And, while I was home, I got a job with Delta Airlines with my close friend, Steve Dawson. Only a couple of weeks into the job, I got picked to go to America with the Irish national team, which is a great honour, to represent your country at any sport and I was chuffed to bits. There were two tournaments, one in Florida, and one in Atlantic City where I'd boxed before.

I'd never been to Florida, so this was a whole new horizon for me, that particular side of America. I'd made my name in New York and the surrounding states, New Jersey, Connecticut, I'd boxed all around there. I'd even made my name on the Canadian border when I fought Lennox Lewis. So this was another side of America that was going to open a door. And it was a great opportunity.

But I'd just started this job with Delta Airline based at Dublin Airport. It was a reasonably new airline into Ireland, and they were only establishing themselves. And they're one of the biggest airlines in America.

I won the title on the Friday night by beating the guy I already told about called Sean O'Regan from Cork, a tough, hard fight and we became great friends afterwards. And, like the normal boxing, you have the greatest of respect for your opponent and you can build up a friendship.

After the fight, I got talking to Art O'Brien who was the Secretary of the Irish Boxing Association at the time.

He said, 'You have been picked to go with the Irish team. We're off to America in 10 days' time. Is your visa valid?'

I said, 'I don't know. It might be, but I don't know.'

'Well give us your passport. Let us get you a visa. You're going with the Irish team.'

'I might not be able to go, I've just started a job.' I was only two weeks into the job with Delta.

'Give us your passport; we'll get you a visa.'

So, as I'm walking through the back of this national stadium I've just boxed, I meet my opponent, Sean O'Regan, coming down the other corridor. So we give each other an embrace. We'd hurt each other, and it was a good fight. So I said, 'I've just meet Art O'Brien, he's told me I'm going with the Irish team in 10 days' time. I might not be able to go, Sean. You're the No. 2, so you're the next choice. Ten days, stay sharp.' In 10 days, you go stale if you don't keep sharp. You go with the team because I might not be able to go.'

And he said, 'Thanks for telling me.'

It was a decent thing to do and I pride myself on it.

That was on the Friday night and, on the Saturday morning, my dad brought my passport up to the Irish Boxing Association for them to get my visa.

Sunday morning, I was in Dublin Airport, and the station manager for Ireland, for Dublin and Shannon, congratulated me on winning my title, which was in all the newspapers. He knew that I'd won my title because on the Friday night, when I was to box, before the fight he joked about me coming into work on the Sunday. 'Don't be getting too marked up coming into work with black eyes!'

I said, 'No one's good enough to put a black eye on me!' The usual banter. Some of the Delta staff had come to watch the finals, and when I arrived that Sunday morning it was the station manager that congratulated me.

I told them, 'I've been picked to go to America on the Irish national team!'

I thought it would be very prestigious for Delta Airlines, but the manager's instant response was, 'Well, you've just started the job; you're only a couple of weeks into your Delta career, it wouldn't be advisable.'

He didn't say, 'Don't go.' He didn't say, 'I'm not allowing

you to go.' But he said, 'It wouldn't be advisable.' I had hoped to hear, 'Go! Delta's blessing! Great! National champion of Ireland, now a Delta employee!' In America, they used a lot of ex-athletes and current athletes to promote the airline. They employed a lot of ex-American baseball players and football players, and they have associated themselves with a lot of sports, and now they had an Irish national champion working in their station in Dublin. The marketing people should have capitalised on it.

I felt sick. I didn't expect them to come out with that at all. And the tone of voice that he said it in, I knew that he was genuine, it wasn't sort of brushed off – 'It wouldn't be advisable at this stage.'

My stomach was sick because I was really looking forward to it – you want to box for your country and you want to box in America, and it's great, the feeling. Win, lose or draw. So I said, OK.

So I had it rolling around in my head – which is more important: your job or your boxing? And, at that stage, my boxing was amateur. I wasn't making any money out of my boxing. Now I've got the chance of a good career. And he didn't say your Delta 'job', he said your Delta 'career'. He emphasised the *career*. There's a lot of people with Delta that have been there years and years and have gone their whole working life with Delta. It's a big, big airline, one of the biggest in America, probably one of the biggest in the world, and they do have great prospects. It was a lovely job working in the airport.

I had to decide which was more important at that moment and to stay home in a good job was more important. My head was trying to rule my heart, and it was stomach churning for me to make the choice. I was doing well with my boxing ambitions. I'd already fought Bobby Wells in '84 who went on to the bronze that year, I was only a young teenager, and in '88 I felt in my prime. I was boxing at a good weight, I was boxing well; I'd beaten the No. 4 in the world, I'd beaten the Polish heavyweight Grzegorz Skrezecz, I'd beaten one of the top fighters in the world, the American Bruce Seldon, and I felt, with the luck of the draw, I could have got to the medal stages of the Olympics in 1984 and 1988.

But on the Monday I contacted the Boxing Association to say that I wouldn't be able to go and they'd already sent the passport off. I'd already given a warning that I might not be able to go, but I got a letter from the Irish Boxing Association asking why I'd handed in my passport trying to obtain a visa knowing that I wasn't travelling with the team? Why did I not give them suitable notification I wasn't travelling with the team? Why did I tell my opponent before I told the boxing officials that I wasn't travelling with the team? Stand before the board meeting and defend these accusations.

So I went mad. I'd won seven Irish titles, I'd boxed for my country a number of times, I'd got a bronze medal in 1987 in the Acropolis Games which is a pre-Olympic tournament – I gave a good account of myself in that, and I lost to the eventual gold medallist Georgios Stefanopolous – so I'd really been a good ambassador for my country, a great ambassador for the boxing and I was fuming. So I said, 'I'm not going to any board meeting and stand before the board to defend these accusations. I've done nothing wrong.'

I felt betrayed, sickened. I felt they'd cheated me out of the Olympics because of my stand after the fight, so now they were trying to discipline me by suspending me for a period of time.

One morning after this, I'd arrived in my old amateur boxing club to train, where I'd boxed for years. And the boxing club said, 'You can't come in to train. The Boxing Association has banned you for a period of time in your absence.'

I said, 'OK, they've banned me, so what? I'm still coming in to train.'

'We have to stand by their decision; you're not allowed to use our facilities.'

'No problem,' I said. I used much worse language than that, like, but I accepted it and I walked away.

I went home, and I was crying with the temper, I was fuming.

Dad said, 'What's wrong?'

'I've finished with boxing, never going to box again.'

'No, no, calm down.'

'No, I'm finished.'

Anyway, Sean had gone away boxing with the Irish team to America and he'd had two hard fights but he got injured in one of them, and there was a home international against Wales a couple of weeks after me being suspended. And they hadn't got a heavyweight to fight this ABA champion. The No. 1 and No. 2 were the only ones that were good enough; the rest weren't really up to scratch for this particular guy.

So they contacted me. They said, 'Joe, the suspension will start after this fight. We've already started the suspension, but we'll start again after this fight. Will you box?'

And I said, 'No.' Not as nice as that, like.

Well, I wanted to call them all the names under the sun. But my dad said, 'No, relax, calm down. Don't let them deprive you of boxing for your country. Don't let them deprive you.'

At that stage, I left my amateur boxing club. The trainer, who was a personal friend, Tommy Mahon, left the club as well, disgusted with the way the Committee had conducted themselves.

I went instead to an amateur boxing club just over the bridge from where I lived, a boxing club called Matt Talbot's. Eddie McCabe was there, a good trainer.

In the end, I decided to fight in the Irish team against Wales, against a guy called Hank Hart who was the finest in the ABA at that time, top-class fighter. But by then I'd built up so much frustration and anger.

I had a different cornerman from my old trainer because now I was boxing for a different club – when you're boxing in a home international, you're allowed to use your own trainers. It's only when you go away in internationals that they bring their national team coaches with them.

And I came out of my corner like a bat out of hell, a bull.

I went straight over at that guy and I smashed him to bits. I stopped him inside the first minute and a half, but during that short time I just battered him to a pulp. I don't think he got a shot off. I had so much anger and frustration because of what they'd done to me – missing two Olympics, the decision against me in the Bernie Deasy fight, the suspension – it was all the anger and I took it out on Hank Hart.

No disrespect to Hank Hart. He was a better fighter than he was allowed to be that night.

And I packed in amateur boxing that night. That was my last amateur fight. I told the whole stadium from the ring! I told Felix Jones, the President of the Amateur Boxing Association. I called him names. I called them all names. The stadium was rocked. They were cheering, because I was always a stadium favourite and I let them know how I was feeling.

I grabbed the mike, and let them know. It was on the radio. I was interviewed on the radio by the radio commentator Timmy McGee who was a personal friend of mine as well. And I told it as it was.

I spoke to Barney Eastwood, because I was going to pack it in.

But my dad said, 'You love boxing. Don't let them spoil your boxing.'

So I spoke to Gerry Storey whose son, Sam Storey, boxed professional – he won the British super middleweight title. I said to Gerry I was interested in carrying on boxing, but, as the Amateur Association had messed me about, I'd go professional. And I went professional then.

CHAPTER SIX

Going Pro

ULSTER HALL

I went professional in January 1990. My manager was Barney Eastwood, Barry McGuigan's old manager. The headlines in the *Daily Mirror* read 'BARNEY SIGNS UP BIG JOE'. I've always been known as Big Joe. Training was at Eastwood's gym in Belfast. He had a stable of champions at the time: Barry McGuigan had been his champion; Dave Boy McAuley – the world flyweight champion; Paul Hodgkinson – the world featherweight champion; Victor Cordoba – the world super middleweight champion; Crisanto Espana – the world welterweight champion. They were all his current champions. And Steve Collins who went on to become super middleweight and middleweight world champion.

In the 1990 WBA Convention in Panama City, it was classed as Europe's most promising gym, or the best gym, conferred by Gilberto Mendoza, the WBA President. I was on the television that year, on the Gerry Kelly show as being the heavyweight prospect from Europe's top gym.

For my first pro fight, Paddy Burns was the matchmaker. Now Paddy Burns's sister Cynthia Burns is my auntie, she's married to my mum's brother, Sean. Paddy Burns is a top international matchmaker from Dun Laoghaire in Co. Dublin; but he works out of Denmark now for Morgens Palle.

He's worked out of London with Terry Lawless and with Frank Warren, Mickey Duff, all the major managers and promoters.

He's a top international matchmaker. And he was making the match for Eastwood. If anybody should have had an easy baptism, it should have been me because his sister's my auntie!

I was now Eastwood's new heavyweight signing. I'm not saying I was the glamour boy of Irish boxing, but I was the character of Irish boxing. I could fill any amateur venue in Ireland just with doing my Muhammad Ali shuffle and my antics, it was fun. But now it's business, and the fun factor's gone.

I was matched originally with a Scottish fighter called Doug McKay then I was matched with a Welsh fighter called Chris Coughlan. And, for one reason or another, whether they weren't happy with the money they were getting, with the rounds or with coming into Ireland, both fights fell through.

Now he's finding it difficult to match me. So now he's matched me with a guy called John Williams, who's coming off two good knock out wins. He's knocked out one of the guys that stood with me in the pub battle, my friend John McBean. And he knocked out Sam Storey's brother – Gerry Jnr, also my friend. I used to spar with Sam in Eastwood's gym. Sam was the British super middleweight champion.

So he's on a roll. He was Herbie Hide's sparring partner; he'd fought at the top level, and he'd gone a number of rounds with experienced fighters. This was my first pro fight, but the adrenaline was pumping. I was ready. I also needed the money!

The fight was in the Ulster Hall in Belfast, 21 February 1990. My dad got me my family crest ring made, with the date of the fight engraved on it, as a present for my first pro fight. Steve Dawson and loads of my friends from Dublin had come up on the coach to watch. Friends and family in Belfast had come. The place was packed. It was a major venue for boxing. I'd watched all the McGuigan fights that had been held there on television.

The plan originally was for me to fight guys that wouldn't have been too hard. Now I'm in against a fighter who's been a top-class operator, 10-round fighter, who's been around a long time, and experienced campaigner. I'm only a six-round fighter, because it's my first fight. And I was going from boxing three rounds to six rounds.

One commentator says, 'It's a big step, three rounds to six rounds,' and Dave McAuley says, 'Joe's full of heart and stamina.'

I was fit. I don't drink, I don't smoke, and I'd got myself in good shape. It was a good action-packed fight. And I'm winning the fight.

Round five, I'm starting to tire.

Tony Baker, one of Eastwood's right-hand men, is doing the Williams corner with Paddy Burns. So I've got my aunt's brother and my manager's right-hand man in my opponent's corner advising him on how to beat me up.

The TV cameras come in close as they're telling him what to do. Tony Baker shouts up to John Williams and Paddy Burns, 'You're behind on points!'

And John Williams looks down. 'I know I'm behind. I'm going to fucking hurt him now.'

He's coming alive now, round five. I'm getting tired. He's a 10-round fighter. He's only getting warmed up, but I'm getting tired. And I'd given it my all!

At the end of round five, Barney Eastwood was giving me my pep talk in the corner in one ear, and Paul McCullagh is giving me a pep talk in the other. But I'm tired, and now I'm on adrenaline and instinct. I haven't punched myself out but I've given him my best shots and he's still there. So I thought to myself, 'One last push. Round six. One more round.'

I went out for one last push and I walk straight into an unmerciful right hand, and it caught me on the chin and I hit the deck.

And it's only my second time being on the deck in my whole career. I've gone on to the ropes a few times, I've sat on the ropes, but I'd only ever been put down once before – by the Greek Georgios Stefanopolous in 1987. In that fight, I was already blinded because my eye was damaged and I didn't see the punch coming and I hit the deck. I got back up, but the fight was stopped at the end of the second round.

But this punch, I could see it coming and I walked straight into it. Bang. Right on the chin.

I jumped up, but my legs had gone. I grabbed John Williams and I'm holding on to him for dear life. A crowbar wouldn't have got me off him. You could not have separated me from John Williams. I was holding on. And I'm shaking my head, thinking, 'Jesus Christ, what a shot!'

In slow motion on the television, when the fight's over, and you see my chin. Bang!

John Williams isn't the hardest puncher in the world. I've been hit by harder punchers than John Williams and they didn't put me down. He just caught me. Bang!

Anyway, I get up and Dave McAuley's commentating and he shouts, 'Hang in there! You can win on points!'

Hang in there? The referee was trying to get me off him! There was no way I was letting go, no way, not for the first half a minute – I've still got a couple of minutes to go! So I'm holding on. The referee's saying, 'Let him go!' but I'm holding on. You're hanging on till you get your head together. And he's trying to get going! Somehow, I fight on, until I hear the final bell.

After the fight, John Williams is leaning on the ropes, sorry the fight was over! He'd have loved another three or four rounds! He'd have really given me stick. He was only getting it together before it was over. Thank God, it was only six rounds.

It was like a bar-room brawl. I've been in some great humdingers, but that was the humdinger to beat them all. The hall's packed to capacity – standing ovation. It was a great fight.

And after the fight I'm screaming, 'Yeah!' Because I'd hit the deck. Because I'd got up. Because Barney Wilson the referee raised my hand. And it's just, 'I've won!'

And I walked over and hugged Barney Eastwood, because the man had looked after me very well. Then I hugged Paul McCullagh, my trainer and great friend.

After, when they showed the slow-motion replay, it showed where I dropped my guard. McAuley was saying they'd warned me in the gym about ducking in. They were saying, 'He tends to take more than he connects with trying to land his shots.' And Dave McAuley was saying, 'We've been trying to work on Joe's defence in the gym.'

Then they were all talking about me hitting the deck, and what a cracking shot, what a brilliant shot it was.

But I'm in the ring and I'm screaming with joy. It was fantastic.

A SPECIAL BREED

It was Dave McAuley's world title defence against the American Louis Curtis, and my second pro fight. I'd watched them on the telly in America, in England and in Ireland. But I'd never actually been to a world title fight. And the first time in my life going to a world title fight, I'm boxing on the undercard!

I fought Carlton Headley – who went on to be the Gladiator 'Raider'. I won the fight on points but I got badly cut. And after the fight I had to go up and get stitched up. I can't remember how many, 54–58 stitches, I got ripped across the bottom, across the top, across the side, a lot of stitches. All across the bottom of my cheek, internal stitches, top of the eye, two or three bad cuts. On the video, you can see the blood pumping out of me.

After the fight, Greg Steen and Alec Steen, who did Carlton Headley's corner, said, 'Anywhere else in the world, the fight should have been stopped!' But because it was in Belfast and I was an Irish fighter they let it go to the final bell.

Paddy Burns is one of the best cutsmen in the world. During my second fight, I'm bleeding heavily. Barney tries to stop it but opens the cut worse than it was. Paddy Burns jumps on to the ring apron to attend to my cuts and pushes Barney Eastwood back. He just jumped up because I'm his sister's nephew, we know each other, and he's my friend. So he's jumped on to the ring apron to help. He's there in an official capacity, as matchmaker, but he's also got a couple of fighters on the undercard, so he's there with his surgical gloves on and everything.

I was ripped apart. The more I got cut, the more my opponent went for the cut. That's boxing, you go for where your opponent's wounded. But I won. I won the fight on points.

After the fight, I spoke to Greg Steen and Alec Steen and they're saying, 'You've got some heart, you've got some heart, you're cut to ribbons and you're still fighting.'

I wanted to get the stitch job done as quickly as possible, so I could get down to see Dave McAuley's fight. So I'm upstairs waiting to get stitched up. But, because the wounds were so severe, they had to go and get a special doctor, not just the doctor that was in attendance. They wanted me to go to the hospital.

My first time at a world title fight! I'm not going to go to the hospital to get seen to. I'm not going to miss this fight!

I said, 'No way! I'm not going! I want to see this world title fight! Stitch me up here!' So, although they were severe cuts, they did it there.

When I get down to the ring – because it's taken so long to do the stitches – I've missed a couple of fights before Dave McAuley's.

Now my dad had watched the Barry McGuigan fights on television with me years before and we used to enjoy the Belfast fight fans. 'Here we go, here we go, here we go!' He used to really love it. He used to get so excited. 'Here we go! Here we go! Here we go!' He'd say, 'It's the atmosphere, son! The atmosphere!'

Anyway, I'd been given ringside seats. When you fight, you get two tickets, as part of your purse.

So, when I eventually come down, Dave McAuley's been announced, and his entourage is carrying the belt into the ring.

And my dad is standing on the seats. 'Here we go! Here we go! Here we go!'

I'm looking at my dad, my eyes all stitched up. I said, 'Dad, what are you doing?'

'The atmosphere, son! The atmosphere! It's electric!'

And it was.

I reached out as Dave McAuley went by and I touched him. He's the champion of the world, flyweight champion of the world. And I touch him.

Now I've been in the gym with him for three weeks before, and sitting at the table eating with him, travelling in the minibus with him, flicking him in the ear, messing about, playing games. But, on the night, I couldn't get close enough to him.

He went into the ring and he boxed and he won his defence of the world title. And it was an honour to fight on his undercard; it was an honour for me to be his friend. But on that night, my first time ever at a world title fight, I boxed and I won on the undercard.

And I just reached in, through the entourage, the trainers, the minders, the people holding his belt, and touched him. I touched Dave McAuley.

To me, world champions are gods. I love the sport, I love the boxers, and champions of the world are a special breed. Every boxer dreams about it. I dream about it.

Even kings dream about being world boxing champion.

DISASTER STRIKES

I was supposed to stay in Belfast after the fight because there was going to be the world title party afterwards. But, because I was so badly wounded and cut up, I didn't want to go to the party. So I went back to Dublin on the bus that my sister had organised for family and friends to come up to watch the fight.

As we're going back on the coach, we're dropping different people off. My sister was studying to be an accountant at the time, and she was doing her accountancy course in college, so she was mixing with potential doctors and solicitors and stuff. Professional people. And we're after dropping off a friend of my sister's, Dr David Mitchell, on Dorset Street.

Five minutes later, we turned on to Parnell Square and we've stopped at the traffic lights, and Lisa, my girlfriend at the time, had parked her vehicle there. We were standing at the front of the coach to get off and the lights went green. Tony the driver said he'd drop us at the next set of traffic lights to save us a bit of a walk. As we're going through the green lights in first gear, a black Mercedes taxi broke the lights from the right-hand side and went into a skid. My granddad who wasn't going back to my house was standing up to say goodbye, and he turned round and shouted, 'It's going to hit us.' It hit us from the side. The Mercedes car went into a skid, lifted the coach the width of the coach again. As I grabbed hold of Lisa, because she would have been thrown against the windscreen of the coach as we were standing, I lost my footing and my leg twisted and the bone in my knee damaged. I'm already stitched up from the fight. I've got 50-odd stitches in my face and, as I fell back, I've hit my jaw on the rail of the arm of the chairs, and I've dislocated my shoulder and cracked my jawbone. So I'm lying on the coach with my arm gripped around her throat. I wasn't unconscious, but I was well stunned. I remember people trying to loosen my grip because I was strangling her. I'm looking up, I'm all dazed.

Then I woke up in hospital.

I'm lying in hospital and they're attending to me. Now we had that accident at five past four in the morning coming back from Belfast after the boxing and we're after dropping Dr David Mitchell off five minutes before.

Eight o'clock in the morning, who comes on duty at the hospital? Only Dr David Mitchell. He couldn't understand it. The night before he'd been on the coach where there was a great, happy atmosphere. He comes on duty for work the following morning, and the passengers that had been on the coach, people he'd said goodbye to a few hours before – my granddad, my brother and others – are now lying all around injured! The passenger of the taxi was also badly injured.

The guy that crashed into us was a taxi driver rushing to get a passenger to the train and we were on the coach with a professional driver. Two professional drivers, on empty roads. I couldn't take it all in. I'm looking at a boxing career finished as a result of two professional drivers being in a collision. I couldn't understand it at the time. It was awful. I got very depressed.

I put on a bit of weight down to depression, down to everything else. Delta Airlines contacted me while I was in hospital and, after a number of weeks, while I'm still recovering, the station manager, contacted me to say they wanted me back at work.

I said, 'I'm on crutches. I've got a cast on my leg. I can't. I'm in no condition to come back to work.'

I was a customer service agent assigned to security. My main job was security – to vet passengers going on to the plane. I had two and a half years with Delta Airlines, a commendation for being an excellent employee, and I was always punctual. I had commendation letters from passengers. I was Federal Aviation Authority registered. I'd had to go over to Atlanta for five days to be vetted by the Atlanta FAA to make sure that I was of proper character. We had what was known as 'selectees', passengers that warranted extra security than the X-ray of the baggage; they also warranted a personal hand search of the bags. They were generally passengers that had been in and out of Palestine, Lebanon, you know, places that were at loggerheads with the Americans. And we X-rayed all the bags, but we also hand searched their bags, asked them questions: 'Had the bags at any time been out of their sight? Had they packed their bags themselves?'

He said, 'We'll sit you on the X-ray machine.' He was determined to get me back to work even in the state I was in, in my hospital bed!

Letters were going in from the doctors. In the end, he phoned me up and he said, 'Your employment with Delta is now terminated.'

I said, 'You lying bastard! You advertised in the programme my professional fight! I've got the copy from Eastwood. "Joe Egan, Delta Airlines, wants to see his boxing career take off like a Delta aircraft."' It was live on television promoting Delta! 'Joe Egan started his job with Delta Airlines.'

I'd even done the travelling trade fair at the Point Depot dressed up as an American baseball player with the managing director of American Express and his family to promote Delta Airlines.

So I took them to the industrial tribunal, where he tried to say it was Delta's policy not to allow Delta employees to have a second job and that they had to try and cover up the fact that I was a professional boxer.

I exposed them in court and I won. But I didn't even take the money that I won. I wasn't looking for any money, just to prove that I wasn't wrong. I didn't want their money after that. It's still with Delta Airlines.

After winning in court, it sort of gave me a bit of a buzz again, a bit of a boost again. I was now gone from being wounded and injured and feeling sorry for myself to feeling good about myself again. So I started back training again. And I took another fight.

I was still on Barney's books, and there was a pro show in Dublin. It was in 1991. Steve Collins was coming back from America to fight Danny Morgan in an eliminator for the world title. Plus it was at the national stadium which is owned by the Irish Amateur Boxing Association, the only stadium in the world owned by the Amateur Boxing Association of any country. And the professional show was being held in the stadium and I wanted to go back there to box professionally because of the treatment that they'd given me as an amateur. I wanted to go back there boxing as a pro but my face hadn't healed up properly, even after all this time, over a year, as those cuts against Carlton Headley were that severe.

I boxed a guy called Denroy Bryan. He was a good fighter. He'd gone a good few rounds with James Oyebola in a fight for an eliminator for the British title and I was winning the fight. I was doing really well. But my face had gone soft. The wounds hadn't healed properly. In the fourth round, I was battering him – his corner later told me he wasn't coming out for the next one – but I got cut at the end of it. I was annoyed because it was a deliberate headbutt. He knew I was weakened around the eyes. He obviously knew about the cuts from my last fight.

The referee – Freddy Tiedt, who was my friend – took me to the corner for the doctor to examine my eye and he said, 'I'm going to stop the fight.'

I felt gutted, because I knew I could have continued. I've had worse cuts. I was winning the fight. I was in front of all my home fans, my family and my friends. And you just feel sick. You feel like you've let everybody down. And the people that you've let down are close family and friends, but also you've given the knockers and the begrudgers something to gloat over.

And depression set in again.

I've come back in front of everyone at home and I was winning the fight, but because of a cut I'm stopped. Because my other two fights had been in Belfast and also in the Kings Hall, it had been homecoming to Dublin as a professional boxer. I felt like I was a failure.

It was very, very hard to accept and I went into major depression. No one can say anything to you. You just feel totally let down. I wasn't a nice person to be around at the time.

INSURANCE CLAIM

I had a big insurance claim coming through as a result of the car crash. Two professional drivers, and I was injured, badly injured. My career was destroyed. But after about a year I was desperate to box again. I was advised by different people that it could lose me a lot of money in the claim. Because, if I had finished and never boxed again, that claim would have been worth an awful lot of money. But I wasn't mercenary, I wasn't money-motivated in boxing; I loved boxing, the money was a bonus.

And, when Steve Collins was having the boxing bill in Dublin against Danny Morgan, I thought what an opportunity to box proud in Dublin in the national stadium where I'd been the top amateur fighter, and against different people's advice I boxed.

I hadn't boxed in over a year because of the injuries received from the car crash. In my previous fight, I'd had severe cuts to my face, with over 50 stitches in my face, and, even though it was over a year before, those wounds it hadn't really healed enough to take a full force punch.

But I boxed. The cuts open again, the fight's stopped. And I lose.

At that stage, I realised that my boxing career was genuinely over. Now I've got to look for another avenue of earning money other than the doors. The doors were to subsidise my income, and I enjoyed the door work when it was a bit of fun, but now suddenly the doors have become my only income. And I've got to try and collect as much as I possibly can out of the claim. And I was entitled to an awful lot of money.

I'd been getting more and more depressed as a result of my boxing being finished. I'd gone into a downward spiral. Because everything I'd ever done was to benefit boxing. Now it was a reality I could never box ever again. In my mind, it was over. So I wasn't concentrating on the claim and I had just let the solicitors run their course.

We'd used a firm called Collier & Co, Joe Collier being the head solicitor, the owner of the firm, who was a personal friend of my dad's. It turned out that Joe Collier's father had died and left him a chain of hotels. So Joe had now gone from being a solicitor with his own firm to running his dad's hotels that he's inherited. One of the solicitors that was in Joe Cogan's practice, a guy called Maurice Jones, had now become a partner, and it was called Collier Jones & Co. Eventually it became Jones & Co, Solicitors.

When I went to that particular firm, I went because of Joe Collier; I didn't know Maurice Jones. So I checked with Maurice Jones. As far as I was aware, everything was running to plan. I learned to my shock that Maurice Jones had been under investigation from the Law Society for some skulduggery and the Law Society has closed him down, for I don't know what reason.

So now I've got a solicitor who's handling my claim suddenly gone out of business. So I try and find out what's happening with my claim and he hadn't even issued the writs. The statute of law in Ireland is that you've got three years to issue the writs and, as he never issued the writs, I'm now looking at a situation where I've no claim coming through from my coach crash.

It turned out that two guys that weren't even on the coach had had claims paid. They'd been up to my first fight, but they hadn't gone to the second fight. These two particular flyboys had got a claim in for the coach crash that they weren't even on. They were advised in this scam by a bloke that knew a bit about being a solicitor without the title of solicitor. This fellow knew the laws inside out and had advised these guys on how to get the claim without actually being on the coach, and both of these guys had had substantial claims. And here's me, a man that had been genuinely injured, career ruined, couldn't get his claim.

So now I've got this on top of everything else, which was terrible and it was very, very hard to accept.

I contacted another solicitor, a guy called Tom O'Reilly, who had handled the claim for other members of the family that had been on the coach. So the insurance firm was aware of passengers that were genuinely injured on the coach. So it wasn't like I'd suddenly just come out of the blue and claimed on a case that they knew nothing about.

But Tom O'Reilly said, 'No, sorry, you haven't a leg to stand on.'

Literally, because my leg had been damaged in the accident.

CHAPTER SEVEN

Birmingham Blues

PADDY FINN TO THE RESCUE

I was getting depressed. Very, very depressed. Boxing had been my world, it had been everything. If I had sex with a woman, it was to give me more stamina for boxing. If I cycled a bike, it was to give me stamina for boxing. If I went walking or swimming, it was for stamina for boxing. I was totally blinkered and focused on boxing. It was my world. I just wanted to box. And when I couldn't box any more because of the coach injury and my cuts problems, and depression, I didn't know what to do.

I had a couple of counselling sessions, but at the time I hadn't got the money to have individual counselling so I had group counselling – which meant I was listening to other people's problems and I was taking theirs on board as well! There were six or seven of us getting the counselling up in Belfast and by the time they came round to me I was really shattered by listening to all their problems, so I took them on top of mine. So that didn't really help me. I was getting more depressed!

I had to deal with it on my own, no matter what my dad and my mum said, even though they are two very inspirational people in my life.

I couldn't accept having lost in those circumstances. Some people, loss makes them come back better. But I thought to myself, 'The cuts – you know, even if you looked at me, I was gonna cut', my scar tissue was that fragile, and I just couldn't accept it.

I was working at the time in Belfast, doing the doors, for a friend called Frank McCullagh. Frank could see my depression and my weight going on and he said to me he was going over to Birmingham to visit an old friend of his, a guy called Paddy Finn, who was an even older friend of mine. (None other than my old hero!) His dad, John 'Boxer' Finn, had founded Donore, the amateur club I boxed for in Dublin. Paddy was the heavyweight champion out of our club years before. Me and him were great friends. And he'd gone over to Birmingham and established himself as a businessman in the pub trade.

So I went over to visit him in Birmingham with Frank McCullagh. We went to his pub in Digbeth, the Dubliner, and there was a big hug and embrace. Paddy had read about the fight, he knew about the loss and about the car crash. And he said, 'What happened to you after your fight?'

I said, 'I just got depressed.'

And he said to me that he had to retire from boxing

because of a trapped disc in his back; he'd had surgery on his back and he showed me the scars. When he'd had to retire, he'd found another business and he knew there was a life after boxing, and that's what I couldn't accept up until that moment in time. I couldn't understand that there *is* life after your boxing career is over.

Paddy Finn said to me, 'There's life after boxing. Come on over, work for me in the pub, and a couple of years down the road you'll have your own pub.'

So I went back to Ireland, and I spoke to my dad about it. My dad said, 'Well, I leave it up to yourself.' The same as myself, my dad had the greatest of respect for the Finns – Paddy Finn and his dad, John. And he said, 'You're going with fine people and he won't see you wrong.'

And then I decided to move over to England.

LISA

In 1989, I was working the door in a nightclub called Blinkers Nightclub up at the Leopardstown Racecourse. Every time I came home from the States, I always got door work, just to help make ends meet when you come home. And I used to come backwards and forwards from America for different boxing championships and for different reasons. Anyway, I was working the door this particular night and I noticed this very attractive young woman in the nightclub. She was with her friend, who turned out to be Margaret. And, when the rose sellers came into the club, I actually sent over a rose to her.

I said, 'Just say it's from a man who would like to take her out.'

Anyway, we'd had eye contact through the night, so the ice was broken with the rose. I got chatting to her. I asked her if I could drive her and her friend home. They said, yeah, they were living in Ballinteer, and it was only 10–15 minutes' drive. So after the club had closed, I dropped her and her friend home. I dropped Margaret off first. Myself and Lisa pulled up and we just chatted and chatted, for hours. I talked about America and the boxing, and it turned out that I knew her cousin, John, who was a doorman in a nightclub called Marny's up the road. And we just seemed to hit it off. She was a lot younger than me, she was only 17 at the time and I was in my early twenties. So I thought I'd go and check with her mum and dad if it was all right if I could take her out. Anyway, she was doing modelling at the time and she invited me to one of the modelling shows to go and watch her on the catwalk. So I said I'd love to go along.

And I met her mum and dad that night when I watched her doing her modelling. She'd told her mum and dad that she'd met this particular doorman. At the time I was driving a nice car, I had a really nice car, a BMW, which is a prestigious car. And, when I met her mum, she said to me, 'You know you're a nice guy!' Surprised, like, because she said the first thing Lisa had said to her was, 'I've met a guy that's doing the door in the nightclub. Wait till you see his car!'

And the writing should have been on the wall then.

We started courting and we courted for a number of years. Then we got engaged.

When I started professional with Barney, I moved up to

Belfast, and Lisa moved up with me and we bought a house just outside Belfast in a place called Crumlin out by the international airport.

There was more money on the doors at Belfast. Plus I'd got a bit tired of Dublin because the scene was very drug-orientated at that time because of the rave scene and I was a bit disillusioned because the drugs had gone from being on the street to now being in the clubs. I'd had my battle with the drug dealers.

She was happy to move too. I was infatuated.

She's a very, very attractive woman and we had some really nice times. But, because I'd had the accident, my boxing career had sort of gone down the pan; I'd made a comeback in my third fight and I lost, and I got very, very depressed. And it was difficult.

She was still young and wanted to go out and enjoy herself, and I didn't really want to go out. But we were still together, we were engaged.

On 30 June 1995, Lisa's brother was killed in an accident. I'd been courting her for a number of years and her brother was a close friend, as were the family. I had done my bit of mourning before going over to England, but she wasn't coming over to live with me because she felt that she had to stay with her family. So I accepted that. I wasn't going to force her to come with me.

In September '95, I moved over to Birmingham to manage Paddy Finn's pub. I did two NVQ certificates, a BII certificate (British Institute of Innkeeping) and I became the licensee of the Dubliner.

So now I've got my licensee certificate, which was great; it was a really good feather in my cap, and I was managing Paddy's pub, the Dubliner, and I was doing ever so well, and had renewed acquaintances with some of my old friends from the boxing scene in Birmingham, some of them well-known names in boxing circles and good friends. And things were going really, really well.

Lisa was still living in my house in Ireland; she was driving my car; I was still sending money home for her to pay the bills at home, but unfortunately she wouldn't come over and live with me until she felt that her family could cope without her. And I felt that her family needed her at that time more than I needed her. But at the same time, I didn't want to lose her, and it's very difficult to keep a long-distance relationship going. And gradually she was coming over every couple of weeks, then it was every month, then it was every six months.

'ME AND YOU OUTSIDE, STRAIGHTENER!'

So I'm in Birmingham, I've done my NVQs, I've done my BII certificate, I'm the licensee of the pub, a very, very successful pub. I'm in a position of trust with my friend. It was great.

Anyway, one particular Sunday afternoon, like any normal pub, it's very busy. It's got two big video screens, one each end of the pub. There's a match on, Gaelic match or whatever, Irish football match. So the pub's packed and it's buzzing. It got a lot of trade passing through from the coach station. This group of about 15 guys had come in. They turned out to be a Midlands kick-boxing team that had been on tour up and down the country and they'd come back to Birmingham. So they come into the pub and they're on a high from their kick-boxing matches. Anyway, they'd spread out around the pub because there wasn't much room for 15 of them to stand in one group. Four were stood at the bar and they were a little bit boisterous, because they were getting the drink quicker than the rest were, because they were standing at the bar, so they were downing it pretty quick. And the more they downed, the more boisterous they got.

So I'm watching. I thought to myself, 'This is all I need; there's at least 15 of them, trained fighters, kick boxers.' Paddy Finn's out somewhere, having a meal or whatever. I thought I don't need this. I've just landed on my feet again, NVQs, my licence, everything's gone well. So I thought I don't need them to start a row, doing their kung fu, kick-boxing moves. So I walk over and I said to the one guy standing there with his muscles and his big neck and all, 'This is a lovers pub not a fighters pub, calm down, lads.'

He gave me a sort of look of contempt, but he said nothing. So I sat more or less opposite them. Rather than walk away, I sat opposite them. Not staring at them, but close enough if they started messing about again I could get at them quick.

At that stage, two girls who'd come off another coach came in to the pub – Tina Brennan and her friend just back from Blackpool or Brighton. 'Hey, Joe,' they said and they sat down beside me.

I thought, 'I don't need this, I'm trying to watch these four, and the two girls are trying to chat to me.'

The two girls are attractive girls and, at that moment, one of the four guys from the bar comes over and he says, 'Move up there, let me sit in beside you.'

I said, 'No, you stay in your own company.'

And he just looked at me, the same contempt as earlier. He said, 'I'm going to blow you away.'

Now I didn't come over from Ireland to be listening to this from some upstart. I thought to myself, 'No, I'm not having this.' So I stood up and I put my arm round him. 'You're leaving now. I don't have to listen to this. You're leaving.'

And, as I put my arm round him to usher him out, he's done some sort of kung fu move, turned and blocked my hand. So, as he's done that, I come up with the uppercut. It was a peach. Bang. Out for the count. His three friends at the bar – four punches, four knock outs. Bang – bang – bang – bang. And the four of them hit the deck. And I looked up, because don't forget there's at least another 10 of his friends in. So I look at them, and they're looking at me. I didn't push the issue. I didn't attack them.

A couple of bar staff helped me carry the unconscious lads outside. And it's like a Clint Eastwood movie, they're lined up outside.

Nealy, Sean Junior and Emmet were at the bar, and they said, 'We've never seen anything like it, Joe.'

I said, 'Ah, it's nothing.'

'Jesus, Joe, what …?'

'No, don't be talking about that. I want to talk about boxing. That's not my scene street fights.'

Paddy Finn came back and I explained to him. He was laughing. He said, 'Well, you weren't the heavyweight champion for nothing.' He's just a great character.

For days, it was all the talk. 'You want to see Joe Egan's punch.'

I said, 'Don't be saying them things. I'm not over here to street fight, my boxing career's finished.'

How glory is short lived!

Always in my whole life when I've been in situations like the gun battle – which I'll tell about later – and other times when people have tried to stab me, or I've been attacked with different weapons – I've always maintained, over my career, somebody watches over me. I believe – in my heart and soul, I know – my grandparents, my mum's parents and my dad's parents, or somebody I've befriended over the years, I believe they watch over me. They're my guardian angels. Somebody watches over me from heaven.

The following week there was a boxing team over and a soccer team over from Ireland because Paddy Finn sponsors all the teams. And they'd had their match on the Friday night at the boxing and their match on Saturday at the soccer. So they're going home to Ireland on the Sunday evening and they're in having their breakfast Sunday morning. So I'm leaving them to have their breakfast and having a chat and I've gone out for the newspapers with my dog, Sheba, a boxer –

naturally! I had her fourteen years before she had to be put to sleep.

As I'm walking down at the front of the bus station, there's a bus shelter and there's a young lad who's got an old man pinned to the ground. There's another lad standing there and a girl, and he's screaming, 'Ballymun!' which is a part of Dublin. So I'm looking at this old man, you could see the fear in his face. The young man's only about six stone dripping wet. So I pick him up and I grab him and I pin him to the bus shelter and I grab his friends. I said, 'Hold him.' His friend wasn't much bigger, another six-stoner. So he's got him now. The old man was up and his legs were going, he's gone. The kid I've got pinned against the bus shelter is still screaming, 'Ballymun! Ballymun!'

I said, 'Shut up! I'm from Dublin as well. Don't shame us any more than you already have!'

There were people outside the newsagents where I was going to; there was the Roscommon pub across the road – that's since become the Kerryman – Liam and Kevin Fitzgerald had it at the time (Liam O'Connor has it now), and they're just looking on.

'Liam and Kevin,' I said, 'you're watching in broad daylight an old man being mugged and beaten up!'

And they were embarrassed. And the shopkeepers.

I said, 'Are you people just looking, nobody going to help?'

Now I'm only over at this pub a couple of months at this stage. Anyway, I go into the newsagents, get my newspapers, get my dog and I walk back up to the Dubliner. As I walked by on the way back up, the other lad's got this young hooligan pinned to the ground again, and the girl's helping to hold him down. These are his friends!

I look and I'm shaking my head. It's broad daylight, you don't expect to see this on a Sunday morning. So I get back up to the Dubliner and I'm talking with Paddy Finn. I said, 'You're not going to believe this,' and I just told Paddy what happened.

Next of all, Boom! The door's kicked open to the pub, the swinging door, and the young lad jumps in. 'Me and you outside, straightener!'

He's only about 16 or 17 years of age, about six stone. I'm looking, Paddy Finn's looking, the young boxing team and the young soccer team are looking. Well, I grabbed him real quick and I threw him out against the metal rail outside. I came back in, and said that's that. I can't believe it, the cheek of him. Next of all, Boom! The bottom of the door's kicked again and the wooden door panel, which pub regular Christie's hand carved – a beautiful harp and stuff – he's busted it right in. Christie's gone, 'Oh, my door! My door!'

So I'm looking at the door, the young thug's run out and he's jumped the metal railings (which they have outside the pub, to prevent you staggering out on to a main road). He's jumped that and he's standing in the middle of the road. 'Me and you, me and you!'

So I'm going out the door, but Paddy grabbed me. 'Joe, don't go out; the cameras are all over the street.'

So I'm going, 'You come in!'

He's shouting, 'Come out!' And he's in the middle of

this road – cars are dodging him. You wouldn't see it in a movie.

I'm saying, 'Come in! Come in!'

Tommy McGeough, who's come to visit me, is laughing. He's come down from Manchester to see the boxing team on Friday night and the soccer team; he's been friends with me a long time, and we since went into business. He runs to the other door, out into the middle of the road, over the far side of the road, comes up behind the young thug and pushes him into the metal railings. No sooner has he pushed him into the metal railings than I jump out, grab him and hoist him over the fence.

Now he's gone from 'Come out, I'm going to kill you!' to 'Jesus, please don't hurt me!'

And I walk him into the Dubliner and show him the door he's just busted; I'm holding him like a suitcase and hitting his head against it: Bang! 'See, look, will you see what you've done!' Bang!

Christie's going, 'Don't damage it any more, Joe! Don't damage it any more!'

'See what you've done!' Bang! 'See what you've done!' Bang!

'Jesus, please don't hurt me! Don't hurt me!'

'Hurt you?' I've lifted him up. 'I'm going to half kill you.' And I walk through the pub, holding him, past the young soccer team and the young boxing team who are just gaping.

Paddy's gone to me, 'Jesus, Joe, look what the damage he's done!'

I go out the back by the Dubliner in the office with the

hooligan. I'm now going to punish him. Tommy's behind me with Paddy.

Now, don't forget, the week before – four shots bang on target, four major knock outs. Now I've got this young 16-year-old, 6-stone dripping wet, at my mercy.

And Paddy goes, 'Ah, Jesus, Joe, you'll kill him.'

'Kill him? I'm going to flatten him.'

So I've thrown the shot, he's moved his head, and I've missed and smashed my knuckles against the wall.

He's going, 'Jesus!'

I'm going, 'Oh my God, my hand!'

He's crawling along the floor, going, 'Don't hurt me any more!'

I've swung a kick and I slip, down I go, dislocate my shoulder and split my head open. So I'm now writhing on the floor. 'Oooohhh!'

Paddy Finn and Tommy are keeled over laughing. I've swung a kick, I've swung the punch, and neither landed. My hand's smashed, the blood's pumping out of my hand, my head's split, and my shoulder's dislocated.

I'm going, 'Ooohh, Paddy!'

Paddy's rocking with the laughing. He gives the youngster a boot in the arse. He helps me up.

I groan. 'No, no, my shoulder, my shoulder.' I know it's dislocated.

So anyway Paddy's carried this young lad out. Now I've come out, right, I'm dripping blood, because the blood's coming down my head, all through my clothes. The blood's all down my trousers from my hand.

The young boxing team and the young soccer team

were staring in disbelief, as I'm in bits. Not a mark on the young thug.

So I've gone to the hospital. They put my shoulder back in and they stitch my head up and they patch my hand up. So I come back and I'm sitting with Dublin Ronnie and Paddy's dad, Boxer. My dog's sitting beside me and I swear to God I look like I've been through the wars. And I'm having a bowl of soup. I'm in pure agony. Whatever bone I'd hit on the back of my head, every time I opened my jaw, it was hurting me. So I couldn't even open my mouth to sup the soup.

Next, this girl comes in and says, 'Can I talk to you?'

'What do you want?'

'Thanks very much for not hurting my boyfriend.'

Hurt him? I tried to half kill him, I couldn't land a punch on him!

I said, 'All right, thanks, no problem.'

So away she went anyway. That night I couldn't sleep because I couldn't lie on my shoulder, I couldn't put my head on the pillow. So the next morning, Monday morning, the bus station is packed, people going to work and whatever. So I'm up, I haven't slept, and I'm in a bad way. And I walk out of the pub to go down to get the newspapers. And I'm in agony because I've hurt my back as well when I fell down, so I'm walking stiff with the pain.

There was a hamburger stand at the front of the Dubliner, with people eating hamburgers and sandwiches before they go on the bus.

The young lad's sitting on the wall out the front. He jumps off the wall. 'I'm sorry about what I did to you.'

I said, 'Get back, please.'

'I'm sorry, I didn't mean it yesterday.'

'Get back.'

There's people watching, this young kid, me a big man. I go, 'No, don't please.'

'I'm sorry, I didn't mean for that. I'm sorry, I didn't mean you to get hurt.'

'Please don't come near me, go back.' It was like Inspector Clousseau with Cato. I've had enough. 'Go away, forget about it.'

'I'm sorry I didn't mean for you to get hurt,' he said. 'I hadn't eaten for a week. I'm sorry, I was drunk on cider.'

'What?'

'We hadn't eaten for a week.'

I was shocked now. I said, 'You haven't eaten for a week?'

'No,' he said, 'we've come over from Ireland, me and my girlfriend and my friend. We haven't eaten for a week.' And he said, 'The cider hit us harder on an empty stomach. I don't do them things, but it was the only way to get money.'

I said, 'Come in.'

So, as I've walked back into the Dubliner with the young kid, Paddy Finn's there and Paddy goes, 'He's not back for round two, is he?'

'Paddy,' I said, 'I've enough after round one. Paddy, the boy hasn't eaten for a week, or his friend or his girlfriend.'

Paddy says, 'Put them up some food there.'

Anyway, they had a feed. Paddy organised for them to go and meet people that he's helped in the Irish community and stuff like that. They're in their twenties now. And one of the young lads now is working, parking the cars at the auctions, and the other young lad does the security at building sites.

When I got my own pub, the Lyndhurst, the two boys got me the rocking chair.

'You're retired now,' they said. 'You've made it. Sit back in the rocking chair!'

They're good lads, nice youngsters. So I said, all right, so I give the rocking chair to my dad. I'm not ready to retire yet.

When I was in prison, one of the lads called to see Ruth one day up in the Moseley Arms. And they're still thin and fragile looking, about 25 or 26 now, but they're just naturally thin, and he says, 'Any trouble in your pub, I'll be up, just give me a call.'

And Ruth looked at him. She says, 'OK, thanks v ery much.'

As she said when she visited me, 'There's not a good row in him!'

And then I took an interest in the two boys and with Paddy Finn's help got them jobs and got them set up in a place, because I've experienced hunger over the years, times have been hard, and I've had people say to me, 'Joe, I remember when you had nothing.'

I say, 'You don't remember it as well as I remember it.'

And when you hear a boy, 16, saying to you, 'I haven't eaten in a week', because he just can't afford to eat, I tell you what, it brings it home to you pretty quick how life really is.

That particular day that person was watching over me and would not let me land a punch on him. If I'd landed a punch on him, I might have killed him. No matter what punch I threw, I couldn't land. So they were watching over me that day because they wouldn't let me land the punch.

SHOWDOWN AT THE LYNDHURST CORRAL

After 18 months, two years, I got a great opportunity to have my own pub. A good pub had come up in the Aston Villa area, and with my business partner, Tommy McGeough, who was from Belfast, we took over the pub called the Lyndhurst in Erdington.

It was a pub that was doing £1,000 a week and we took that pub to £16,000 a week in a matter of months. We had two boxing tournaments there, and we had a forum with the stars. We had Richard Woodhall, the world super middleweight champion, Bunny Johnson, the first black British heavyweight champion, Rob Norton, the world cruiserweight champion, and Ernie Shavers, who was the hardest puncher ever of all time. They all did forums in the pub.

We had the Lions Club, which is the most charitable organisation in the world, base themselves there. We had the No. 1 ladies darts team in the Midlands, and we had a decent men's darts team. We built the community pub and it was going from strength to strength.

Then in July '98 – almost a year after we first traded – the racketeers, the gangsters, decided the pub needed protection. There was no warning.

They'd burned down two of Paddy Finn's pubs over the years. They'd killed, they'd maimed and they'd butchered. They'd run a particular section of Birmingham for 15 years. They're called the Darcy family. Some are connected with the Aston Villa football hooligans, the Combat 18. All racially motivated.

The Combat 18 is a splinter group of the National Front. Combat 18 stands for Combat 1-8, which is the first letter of the alphabet, A, and the eighth letter, H. It actually stands for Combat Adolf Hitler. So these are a recognised terrorist organisation.

They have a lot to do with football hooliganism. They're sort of scum, for want of another word. They associate themselves with all sorts of violence because they trade on violence, fear and intimidation. So anything that has an element of violence, they want to be associated with it.

It was a protection racket – they wanted £500 a week to not wreck our pub. But also they wanted to prove that they were the big shots, because this was an Irish-owned pub, a pub frequented by ethnic communities, Asian, Chinese, black. People make the mistake thinking that the National Front and the Combat 18 just hate black people. They hate Asians, they hate blacks, they hate Chinese, they hate Irish. They're just a hateful organisation.

I wasn't knowledgeable enough at the time about racism because we didn't experience racism at home in Ireland and I wasn't experienced in what racism was all about. Even though I knew about it, I didn't know enough about it. And my friends at the time warned me, they said,

'Joe, that's a racist area.' But I thought that racism was just against blacks, I didn't realise that the racism was against Irish as well. And, when I took over this pub, it was against a couple of black friends' advice.

But I felt the same as I felt when I was boxing, I was a world beater, there was nothing could stop me. If I was determined to do something and I put my heart into it, me and Tommy could make a go of this pub.

On Sunday, 19 July 1998, they sent a guy called Jake.

In the Irish community, Sunday was family day. We had to be home on a Sunday. Every other day we could pop in and have our dinners at different times, but on a Sunday we all had to be around the table. And it's always been a family day. And it's still to this day in Irish communities. I don't know what it's like in the Jamaican community, but I think it must be similar.

So I encouraged family day in my pub. It used to be crammed full of children. And Danny Brown did the door on the Sunday with GT, not because of trouble, but, because the car park was big, the kids used to go out to the car park, and we were worried about taxis pulling in too fast. Also, there was that many boxers who used to use the pub, ex-boxers and current boxers, we never had trouble. It was the safest pub in England. I used to joke to my bar staff, 'Whatever you do, don't ring that bell for last orders – they'll all leap off their stools and start boxing!

So I'm not boasting but, in my eyes, it was the safest pub in England because of the genuine guys that were drinking in the pub.

Anyway, on 19 July 1998, this Jake Welch came in saying that he wanted to put his doormen on the pub.

So I said, 'No, we don't need any doormen. The pub's running smooth. We don't need doormen.'

He said, 'If you don't put our doorman on the pub, you'll have a lot of trouble with the Darcys.' And he said he wanted to put his men on the door at £500 a week.

Now I knew there were a few faces in the bar, and they weren't regular faces. I didn't know if they were armed, I didn't know what they were.

I said, 'Are you threatening me?' and I've raised my voice.

My two friends, John McBean and Warren Wiggan, both tough guys, were playing pool. They stopped. John McBean comes over. He knows I can't risk losing my licence. I can't afford to be arrested. So he nudges me out of the way.

He says, 'Is this a black thing?' John knew that these guys were racist.

Warren's black and John McBean's black. A lot of black people used my pub at the time. I did a lot of black funerals, and we had a lot of black weddings. The Irish have always had a good rapport with black people, from the sixties.

John's a dangerous man, a tough hard man, ex-professional boxer, well-respected man. Warren's beside him, another well-respected man in the Birmingham community.

Jake Welch was stopped for words now because he suddenly realised that I wasn't on my own. He said, 'No, no, you don't understand.'

John McBean said a couple of other things to him, then said, 'It's best you leave.'

So he's walking out of the bar to the foyer of the pub, and Warren and John are following him out and I'm looking at these others sitting around because John and Warren wouldn't know these others sitting around weren't regulars.

So away goes Jake Welch, and shortly afterwards five or six other people that were sitting scattered about left as well.

John and Warren asked me what it was all about. I told them. Later that day, John and Warren phoned a couple of the lads to come up and have a late drink. They were to go and meet them somewhere else, but they phoned them to say that they were staying.

I said, 'No, no, don't mess up your day.'

They said, 'We'll have a drink in the pub late tonight.'

Next, my business partner Tommy comes back to the pub. I'm sitting at the bar in the lounge at closing time; the day's gone without a hitch, other than the words with Jake Welch.

At closing time, I get a phone call saying, 'You're still open?'

I said, 'Well, we're not still open but there's a few in the pub having a drink.'

I thought it was one of my regulars that were going to come down and have a late drink. People phone me all the time: 'Are we having a stop back?' The law says you're allowed to have people in the pub as long as you're not taking money. So even if I was talking to a policeman I wasn't doing anything illegal.

So I said, 'Who am I speaking to?'

The phone hung up.

So now whoever was on the phone knows that we're still here, but they think it's just me and Tommy.

Suddenly, there's a gang of 10 or 15 hoodlums coming across my car park. Right, so I hear a bit of a commotion out in my car park. So I jump up and there's six or eight lads in my lounge having a bit of a laugh and a bit of fun. So I walk out. At this stage, John and Warren take over and they step outside the door. And these lads were coming across my car park with scarves covering their faces. They see John and Warren and they know now that I'm not on my own. So suddenly they've stopped in their tracks.

'What's going on, Warren?' They know who Warren is.

And Warren and John close my door and have a few words with them.

At this stage, a police car pulls in and the crowd all disperse. A police sergeant gets out. 'What's going on?'

I said, 'To be truthful, I'm not 100 per cent sure.'

I explained to him what happened earlier on in the day. I said, 'I don't know what this was all about.' Because at this stage I didn't see any face that I knew from earlier on. I didn't know at this stage what this was all about. So I liaised with the police through the week because there's pretty much a tense atmosphere all week.

I was a businessman and licensee now. I'd left all that in Ireland, doing the doors, the battles, and everything else, to run a good pub. I'm not a vigilante – I'm a businessman, right. Let the police handle it.

The sergeant was from the local police, a nice guy, he was keeping up to speed on what was going on and they were doing their investigations. I told him all about the protection demand.

There was no trouble from 19 July to the following Sunday, 26 July, when I got a phone call to say that these gangs are gathering in the Yenton and the Norton pubs.

Tommy, my business partner, ex-French Foreign Legion, Medal of Honour winner, he won the Croix de Guerre, is a Belfast man and he's grown up in war because the Northern Ireland situation was a war; he was an ex-martial arts expert, ex-boxing champion, a proper hard man, conditioned hard, trained hard, still to this day, in his forties now, super fit, super strong. He was pensioned off from the French Foreign Legion because he got malaria.

He said to me, 'Let's bring it to them. If they want trouble, let's bring it to them.'

I said, 'Tommy, I'm a businessman.' I'd not gone soft, but my boxing career was over for me. This was my second career, I've got business opportunities. I didn't want this one to be over for me too. 'We're running a good pub, we're making good money, we're making great money, let the police take care of it.

So Tommy says, 'OK.'

So I phoned the police sergeant and told him, 'I've had a phone call these gangs are gathering in the Yenton and the Norton. They're going to attack my pub.'

He said, 'I'm on my way to you.'

The Yenton is up the road, 400 yards from my pub. The man that ran the pub was a friend of mine. Jake Welch was running the doors there, and in a number of pubs in the area, as part of the protection and the racketeering.

Lo and behold, the sergeant says, 'I'm on my way to you. I'm going to radio the station, get them to send men to these pubs to physically walk through the pub to disperse any gangs that are gathering.' These are the sergeant's words to me.

As he's on his way to me, he got a radio call and they sent him to a Mickey Mouse alarm call in the Bromford. Mine was a genuine distress call. It turns out that the armed response unit was ready from two o'clock that day; they knew there was men coming to my pub, with guns. But what did they care? It's a group of black men and a group of Paddies – there for slaughter by the racist thugs.

On that particular day, 26 July 1998, we had a communion going on in the function room. Father Thomas Malloy, who was the priest that was attached to the Abbey Church which was on the same stretch of road as the Lyndhurst, used to bring us up business to the pub. He encouraged parishioners in his chapel to bring their business to the pub – communions, weddings, funerals. He was a Belfast priest and he had done Tommy's communion 30 years before in Northern Ireland. So he had a double reason to bring us business, not just because the church was next door to the pub but also because the man that owned the pub was a family friend. That particular day's communion had been booked months in advance. Now we were aware something was going to happen on the day and I actually encouraged the family to cancel, but they said, if we were going to make a stand, they were going to make a stand by having their function at the pub. The community spirit was that strong.

In the pub that day, there were families, young children, old men, old women. Family pub, packed to the rafters. I also had a few friends inside, ex-boxers. These men were about to put their lives on the line for me.

When the gangs eventually get on to my car park, there are 37 of them armed with a handgun, a shotgun, hatchets and machetes.

I'm in the office making my second call to the police. The pub has 16 security cameras, and the monitor can show pictures from all 16, or eight or four, or only one. It's showing the four main ones – the car park, the inside foyer, the lounge and the bar. I can see the armed gang gathering in the car park, around the area of the cabby rank. They're starting to throw glasses. Many of them have masks and scarves around their faces and various weapons – clubs, sticks, machetes, baseball bats.

With his army swarming behind him, Jake Welch approaches the double front doors, one of which is open. He takes out a silver .32 calibre handgun and starts firing rapidly at the doors. He's wearing no mask or gloves. After three shots, the gun jams; he makes several attempts to fire it, then throws it down to the ground.

People are panicking and screaming and ducking. I'm coming out of the office inside and heading towards the front foyer. Unknown to me, one of his men has now handed Jake Welch an even deadlier weapon.

Jake Welch – no mask – stepped up to the open doorway, up to my door with a shotgun. As I rounded the corner from the office, I saw him entering the bar directly in front of me, with the shotgun levelled. I stepped back immediately behind the wall, pressed back against it, and crossed myself. I'm not ashamed to say I was afraid.

As he stepped into the bar, a good friend of mine, Steve Dalton, an ex-boxer, ran out from the bar screaming, 'Aaaaahhhhh!!!'

Jake Welch looked shocked. The last thing you expect any man to do is to run against a gun!

He pointed the shotgun half-down and let rip the first shot.

Some of the pellets hit the ground and some of them came up and caught this guy in the legs and the arms. He didn't take the full force of the shotgun, but the ricochets caught him.

At this stage, Jake Welch is panicked because, whether his intentions were to wound or whatever, his intentions weren't to do somebody else, his intentions were to do me. At the time, I didn't realise this, but I know it now.

(Remember, I've phoned the police, who are well aware that this attack is happening. In court later, it was established there were four phone calls that I made begging for help).

As I'm looking at my wounded friend, an old man, a guy called Jim O'Brien, steps out with his hands up.

Jim's from Limerick. A good customer and I'd built up a friendship with him. He also lived next door to the Darcy family all their lives, his children had played with their kids, grown up with them, his daughter was living in one of the Darcy apartments, John Darcy's girlfriend was sharing an apartment with Jim's daughter.

So Jim O'Brien steps out with his hands up. 'Please I can stop this. I know these boys.'

At this point, I step out from behind the wall to pull the old man in behind the wall. Jake Welch raises the shotgun now for the second shot. I've looked into many men's eyes over the years from boxing and from rows. I've looked into their eyes, but I've never looked into a man's eyes with pure evil, I mean pure evil like you could not imagine.

And he let rip with the second shot from the shotgun. He blasted that old man to get to me. I was standing behind the old man, and he didn't care. This is an old man who he knew; he blasted the old man in the hip, blew the hip clean out of him. He fell into my arms. Some of the shotgun pellets hit around my arms, and a shotgun pellet punctured my nose, a few all over my body. So I've got the old man now in my arms and he's splattered all over my foyer, bits of flesh and whatever else. He's took a bad blast.

The moment the second shell from the shotgun was gone, the lads that were in the bar and the lounge ran out. I put the old man down to be attended to in my lounge by my bar staff and a couple of my customers.

And I go outside and there's a scene in my car park, right across as far as the eye can see. There's a battle going on. There's a guy cornered and he turns around with his hatchet and he goes, 'Come on.' And one of them sticks the hatchet into his chest. He drops his weapon and he's shaking now. So he's grabbed by the hair, he's pulled down and this guy's trying to chop his head off. And he's going to his face saying, 'Stay still!' He's getting chopped to bits.

Another guy with a bayonet's standing beside this person saying, 'Jeez, you're going to kill him.' This person turns to this other guy. 'Get another one.' This guy that was chopped to bits underneath the tree in the car park had to be brought back to life in my car park. His life was saved in hospital. There was a load of the other gang too badly wounded.

Geoff Darcy, 'Fat Darcy', was trying to climb a wall and he was pulling his friends down as he was trying to climb the wall. These are guys that have stood beside him. He was grabbed by the hair and his throat was cut.

Across the road, there were a couple of guys running. Another couple of lads corner this guy Bobby Darcy, who was an animal. He runs into a dead end lane and turns. A couple of guys that are chasing him have no weapons. He's got the machetes. One decks him with a punch. As he hits the deck, a couple of the lads with the weapons jump on top of him and they sliced the living daylights out of him. It was a bad, bad scene. There was bits of limbs, bodies everywhere.

On a Sunday afternoon, there was a 25-minute pitched battle. The newspaper said it made *Braveheart* look like a Walt Disney movie.

I made my third call to the police for help. The ambulances and the police eventually arrived, after a 25-minute pitched battle, 55 minutes in all after the first distress call.

The Catskills.

Top left: Camilles big house that became a home for us all.

Top right: Camille and I with the 'Sharpei' (*right*) given to Mike when he fought Tony Tubbs in Japan.

Above: Mike Tyson's adopted mother, Camille, a wonderful lady.

Left: The pigeon loft that Mike, Jay, Tom and I built for Tyson's flyers.

Mike Tyson took all 4 photos, house dogs, loft, Camille and Joe.

Above: Mike Tyson with a gift from Tommy and I, a pigeon carved from marble, done by Tommy's brother-in-law, Tony Currie, former Irish Boxing Champion.

Below left: Me, Tom McGeough and Mike Tyson.

Below right: Mike, me and Jay Bright in Mike's training camp at the Grovesnor House Hotel.

"Joe, your friends are my friends."

Above: Mike was happy to meet my friends Jim Rock and James Campbell just before his fight with Julius Francis.

Right: Warren Wiggan (*left*), Bunny Johnson and Mike Tyson.

Below: Bunny Johnson, Mike and Steven Dalton.

Top: Here I am as a guest of Birmingham City football club at, St Andrews, with Man-of-the-Match Damien Johnson.

© Action Images

Above: Nigel Rafferty and me with Tom Scragg Managing Director of Moya Payroll services in our role as security. I think Nigel is one of the toughest men on the planet, 104 pro fights not out.

Right: With Roy Shaw, his book was an inspiration it helped me through my own prison sentence.

© Tony Bowden

Above, left to right: Joe Senior, Scott Welch, Sugar Ray Leonard, me and Jim Rock, Flex Fitness Gym in Birmingham.

Below: Lads' night out, Dubliner pub in Birmingham (*back row*) Jason Dimmock, Flatley look-a-like, Tom Byrne (*front row*) Phil Bell, Paddy Finn, me and Mike Higgins.

Above: One of the men who gave me the inspiration to write a book, Charlie Hale (*centre*) with rugby league star Paul Sculthorpe.

Right: Warren Wiggan, Showtime's Tom Casino and me.

Below: Me showing Lennox Lewis the two-move check mate.

Above: After my comeback fight against Mark Williams with friends JR Rogerson and his son Steven.

Right: Me and Rocky Graziano. Paul Newman played Rocky in the film *Somebody Up There Likes Me*.

Below: Flying around the world with the Irish boxing team. Sitting with Brendan Lowe, Irish Boxing Champion.

Below right: Proud to wear the green vest for Ireland.

Left: A well protected woman. Ruth flanked by World Boxing Champions, Alan Minter (left) and Steve Collins.

© Alan Shaw

Below: The Night of the Hitmen. *Left to right*: Gerald Gordon (GTN Security), Emanuel Stewart, Alan Minter, Tommy 'The Hitman' Hearns, Ricky 'The Hitman' Hatton and me.

© Alan Shaw

Above: Best of friends. Earnie Shavers, Kenny Rainford, Mike Higgins, Nigel Rafferty and me at Ron Gray's dinner show.

© Alan Shaw

Left: Me on the pumps at the Lyndhurst Pub.

Photo supplied by sports writer Jerry Hjelter

They'd had an armed response unit ready from two o'clock that day. They knew there was men coming to my pub with guns. And the police station's not 400 yards from the pub. You could walk it 50 times in 55 minutes.

Some of the lads that stood and defended the pub with me got showered, freshened up, and were gone before the police arrived.

Because he's my doorman, Danny stayed watching the pub while I had to go to hospital with the old man that was wounded pretty bad, and for my own wounds as well. We got to the hospital in the ambulance. There was a number of ambulances taking bits and bodies away.

As we pull into the hospital, one of the ambulance drivers that had got there first comes out, and he says to my ambulance driver, 'Hey, you're not going to believe this, we've got all the gangs from the Lyndhurst, they're all here at the hospital.'

'What's this about gangs?' I say. 'We're not gangs. I'm the landlord of the pub. We were attacked by a gang. I've got an old man who's shot pretty bad. Is there a police presence in the hospital, as I'm on my own?'

He goes, 'Yeah, yeah.'

We go into the hospital, the old man's taken in on a stretcher and he's being attended to pretty well sharpish.

I'm sitting there and it's so surreal. A couple of weeks before, I'm living the life of a millionaire, and now my bubble's burst. I'm feeling sorry for myself. I'm wounded.

As I'm sitting there, two guys walk by me. One of them, a guy called Terry French, an ex semi-professional soccer player, who used to play for the Sunday League, puts his fingers to my head in the shape of a gun as if he's shooting me in the head. This is the other gang! His brother had been chopped up pretty bad.

This is in the casualty unit at the hospital. So I stand up and knock him and his friend out, sparked the two of them, bang, bang. They hit the deck. I pick up the stool and I go straight at the other people in casualty. They're all bandaged up, and they're all screaming and shouting, 'It's nothing to do with us! It's nothing to do with us!' Because now the panic's taken over again. I'm screaming and shouting because they've walked me into a trap. They walked me into all these families of the people that had been chopped up by some of people that protected me and the families in my pub.

The police begin to arrive. I leave Jim O'Brien to be attended to and looked after, and leave the hospital pretty sharpish.

The next day I attended another hospital and got myself patched up. There's a shotgun pellet in my nose. They said they would have to cut it right open to take it out. I said, 'Leave it in, just take the rest of the pellets out of me.' (The shotgun pellet's still in my nose. I have to be careful when I sneeze, I might shoot somebody!)

Over a period of 10 days, there were all sorts of investigations going on and they closed my pub. Some say it was the police using me as a scapegoat for their negligence, and I wouldn't disagree with them. They tried to revoke my licence. I was charged with attempted murder.

The police station that was handling my business was Queens Road Police Station. Now Erdington was the district where my pub was, but Erdington was a part-time police station and it only opened for a certain amount of hours a day. After a certain time, Queens Road Police Station took over. There was a feeling in the local Irish community that there was an element of racism within the Queens Road Police Station. Not them all, of course, I don't knock all police officers; if you don't have police you've anarchy. My brother-in-law's a cop. So you have to have a police force, you have to have a ruling body; there has to be people to enforce law and order.

Danny was arrested too. He had stayed on the scene because he was my doorman and my friend, to watch my money, to watch my premises, and Tommy's premises, as he was Tommy's friend as well.

Eventually, they dropped the charges against Danny. They agreed to let the pub open again on the condition that it was made to be like Fort Knox with crash barriers, shutters.

The Chief Inspector at the time said that the gang's normal procedure was to petrol bomb because they had burned down a number of pubs. He said the only way he'd let the pub stay open was to fortify it. So I had to have no letterbox and install a steel front door, cameras and crash barriers.

Well, the trade went down, but we built it back up again, because the way we looked at it was that, if these animals didn't get in here, they'd get into other pubs.

We went back down to four and a half grand from sixteen and I was feeling really bad, but my accountant and my friend Ken Pritchard said to me, 'Look at it this way, the first time round when you hit four and a half grand from taking over from a thousand, how did you feel?'

'I felt great.'

'Look, don't feel too bad, at least we didn't go back to square one.'

We went from sixteen down to four and a half instead of sixteen down to a thousand. But the pub needed six grand a week to break even, so we were struggling for a number of weeks until we built it back up. The VAT was due and they gave us a deal. I was the only person in the pub trade known to get a deal out of the VAT. Normally, the VAT look at your cash business, 'You've had *your* money, we want ours', but they gave me a helping hand because I said to them, 'Look, these scumbags that attacked me couldn't beat me; don't you finish the job for them. Don't put me to the wall and put us out of business. If you want to put the nails into the coffin, you close me. If you want to make them successful and make them glorified more than they already are, you finish the job for them.'

They gave me a deal, letting me pay off the VAT due over a period of months, so we were able to use money saved up for the VAT to keep the wages going, to keep on a front that everything was back to normal. And over a period of weeks that is exactly what we were able to achieve.

The staff were sound. The staff stood by us. After what they'd experienced, they were brilliant. They stood by me and did me proud. And it was nice. I used to take them out for Christmas meals, had a good working relationship and a friendship with some of them.

But the most important thing was the customers. There's no point in having any staff if there were no customers. And people that hadn't frequented the pub came and supported me, people that had been seeing this going on for years before travelled from all over the Midlands to come to my pub to show solidarity, to show support.

There was no way the gang were coming back. They'd come to dictate and they'd got slaughtered.

I was fortunate that there were friends with me. There was no other reason to be at the pub. There was men stood beside me in that pub, and women – there's women stood with me as well that day. There's women that attended wounded and there was women helping me, so men and women stood together. United we stand, divided we fall, and that particular day, if me and Tommy had been there on our own, we'd have been dead, I wouldn't be here sitting telling the story now. Both me and Tommy would be dead. They would have killed us, because I wouldn't have bowed to them and Tommy wouldn't have bowed to them, so we would have stood our ground.

We'd have taken a few of them with us, but what good is that?

We had video cameras in the pub, but Tommy was getting golf lessons, and he was using the bloody videotapes to have his golf lessons recorded, so we weren't recording. That's the only day we didn't record!

The police eventually tried to get the court to try to

revoke my licence for attempted murder and everything else. But I beat them in court.

The police sergeant apologised. 'I'm sorry, Joe,' he said, 'I'm sorry.'

I summonsed him. I summonsed the head of the armed response unit who admitted in court that they were ready, that they were aware that there was gangs coming with guns.

I proved that I phoned the police before, during and after, and the Chief Superintendent still tried to close me.

Whatever dislike he took to me, I don't know, I don't understand why, he had no reason to hate me. Maybe he tried to blame me for his negligence. The headlines in the newspapers were 'JUSTICE PREVAILS'.

I beat them in court, but I was warned by a high-ranked retiring police officer, 'Listen, the police will be out to get you. You've embarrassed the police force. You did the job that they couldn't do. My advice is carry a Dictaphone with you everywhere you go. Every time a police officer approaches you, even if it's coming to pat you on the back saying a job well done, switch it on.'

For about six weeks, I carried a Dictaphone with me, in my car, in my pocket. I just got mad paranoia. And it's not me. I'd never been in trouble before.

My grandfather was a retired police sergeant in Ireland. My sister's married to a police officer in New York. With my brother, I was four and a half years in the part-time army at home – which was a second for the military police. A lot of lads I was with went on to join the Irish Police Force. I've never been any threat to the police. I'm not a thug, I'm not a gangster. At the end of the day, I didn't feel that I had to conduct my life like that, it was stupid. So I put the Dictaphone away.

'JOE! IT'S MY NEW CAR!'

After the West Midlands Police let me down in the attack on the pub, they charged me with attempted murder and tried to close my pub and everything else; they took a lot of my personal belongings when they raided the pub, including photographs, which were of sentimental value. When I was arrested, they kept the clothes that I was arrested in. They were covered in blood – my own blood, because of the gunshot wound. Afterwards, when they eventually dropped the charges, I got a lot of these photographs back and I wanted to get my personal belongings back. Eventually, I got a call from the police, to come at 3.00pm the following day to collect my stuff.

I wasn't in any fit condition to drive; I was on crutches, and actually I couldn't even sit down properly. Tommy was away so I got a guy who was using the pub that just happened to come up that day to show his new car. Fair play to him, he's a nice guy. He said he'd give me a lift.

Three o'clock, I'm in the foyer of Queens Road Police Station on crutches. As I'm standing in the foyer, there's three other guys there. I'm looking at their faces and you know the way you recognise them but you don't recognise them. They weren't looking directly at me; they were looking down. Most of the guys that had attacked me on the day were wearing balaclavas and scarves around their faces, so all I'd seen were their eyes. But it was enough. I know it's them.

The door opens and I'm ushered into this particular office. There's two plainclothes and a uniformed officer there. And they give me one sock, one shoe and a shirt.

So I say, 'I've come down to collect all my personal belongings. You're giving me one shoe, one sock and a shirt. Where's all my photographs?'

The plainclothes guy leans in to my face. 'You hardly want your hatchets back, do you?'

I said, 'They weren't my hatchets. I don't know what you're talking about. They're not mine.'

At that stage, the door opens, the uniformed police officer from outside leans in. He said, 'We'd better keep Joe in here. We've got two of the Darcys and a Morgan.'

Three of the bastards that attacked me in the pub – they *were* the three guys that were standing in the foyer! Not only had the police told me to come here at three o'clock, they'd also got the scumbags that had attacked me in the foyer of the police station!

At that stage, I threw the crutches down. I said, 'Let me out!' And I'm trying to get out past the two uniformed coppers that were standing in the room now, one at the door, one beside the door. I've got the two plainclothes officers trying to stop me. I'm trying to get at these three animals, who they're ushering into the room at the same time as ushering me out!

I'd just had surgery, so I wasn't in a fighting state, but there's no way I was going to leave – I wanted these guys!

The police got me out, no sweat, a child could have pushed me out I was so weak. So I'm outside the door now, as the three animals are ushered past. I'm still trying to get eye contact! I just want to look at one of them; I just want to look into their eyes. I wanted to put the fear into them that they put into me on the day of that attack. They wouldn't look at me!

Now I'm outside the room; they're inside, closing the door.

I don't know where the strength came from. I got one sudden burst of strength and I hit the door with my shoulder. The pain, because I was full of stitches from surgery, went right through my body but I'm back in the little room.

I say, 'Did I leave anything in here?'

I was so weakened that the woman police officer ushered me out again. My crutches were handed to me.

Outside the police station, I limped over to the guy that has given me the lift and got into the car. 'Right,' I said, 'there's three of them in there, two of the Darcys and a Morgan. When they come out, ram them.'

'What?'

'When they walk out of that police station, you ram them. Stick them to the wall. Splatter them all over that wall.'

'Oh, Jesus, Joe, what're you on about?'

'Do what I say!'

'It's my new car.'

I said, 'Shut your mouth! I'll buy the car off you! I will pay you for the car! Please smash them against the wall! Stick them to the wall! Let them be scraped off that wall!'

'Jesus, Joe, please!' He breaks down and starts crying in the car. He was crying about his new car. I can't drive and I'm begging him. I'd pay him for the car! Give him the money for the car.

Mad isn't the word. These people had shot me, they'd tried to kill me. I couldn't help thinking the West Midlands Police had brought me down there, thinking that I'm going to be intimidated when I'm on crutches. I'm the same man on crutches as I am walking; I don't get intimidated by that scum.

But I wanted to make a point and I kept on begging him! 'When they walk out of that police station, stick them to the wall! Let Queens Road Police Station be peeling them off that wall! Splatter them all over that wall!'

He's crying about the car: he's begging *me*! 'Please, Joe, leave it!'

I phoned Tommy, who was at the far end of the country. He said, 'Joe, relax, calm down. Don't be worrying about that. Calm down.'

The police have stayed away from the pub, left me to be attacked and to be killed. It seems like to me they've knowingly walked me into the hospital afterwards amongst the men who'd attacked me. Now they've got me going to the police station at the same time with the same animals. Calm down? I was in a fury.

LISA AND THE OTHER MAN

At that particular time, because my business was suffering, my health was suffering too as a result of it all, from the stress. I'd never been in trouble like this before.

To go from never being in trouble to suddenly being charged with attempted murder, you know.

I took very sick. I had an abscess in my bowel that burst because of stress. They didn't detect the abscess and the poison was going through my system. I got yellow jaundice, and I was very, very sick.

I was hospitalised, and trying to run a business and fight the police from my hospital bed. My mother came over, while my business partner was trying to hold things together.

Lisa came over, but she wasn't very helpful or supportive. She showed no inclination to stay and help me through this bad time. If anything, she seemed more concerned about having a second breast enhancement, and she returned to Dublin.

We'd been together for 10 years. I was still sending money to her. I was happy with Lisa. As far as I was concerned, we were going to be together for ever and I didn't think in my wildest dreams that what happened later was going to happen.

She started working, and she was going to college to study to be an accountant technician. This was as well as her modelling. Her friend Rachel had graduated from college as an accountant and was working for the firm that had put her through college. She'd been paid by this firm to go through college on the condition that when she left the college she worked for them. Her income wasn't anything special while she was studying, but between the two of them they could do small businesses' books in their own time. As neither of them was earning much money, I bought them over thousands of pounds' worth of office equipment – computers, faxes, everything – through my business to send home for Lisa to set up an office in the house where they could work for a couple of evenings a week doing small businesses' books.

I'm working 18 hours a day, and I'm also sending her money. I'm paying the mortgage, I'm paying the tax and insurance on her car, I'm paying all the bills and sending her money. She was living the good life.

I paid for her flights to visit me. And, when she came over to England, I spoiled her while she was here. She would come over with empty suitcases, and go back with full suitcases. She wanted for nothing.

This particular day, I phoned her and said, 'I love you, see you on Friday.'

I couldn't get her Saturday, couldn't get her Sunday, couldn't get her Monday. Tuesday morning, I got her. I said, 'Where have you been? I've been trying to get you for days.'

'I feel trapped,' she said. 'I need a break. It's all too much for me.'

I knew then there was something else. Tuesday afternoon, I'm in Dublin.

I've got the court battles going on and at the same time the brewery are trying to evict me because they're saying I'm not a fit and proper person. I'm trying to build the business back up. So now I've got all this to contend with as well.

So I'm in Dublin and I phone her. 'Lisa, I'm in Dublin now. I'm going to sort out money. I want to see you.'

'If you come near my house,' she said, 'I'll have you arrested.'

This is my missus living in my house; we're engaged to be married! Come near my house, I'll have you arrested?

'First of all,' I said, 'what about my money?'

She said, 'Kiera' – that's her sister – 'will meet you in O'Connell Street, give you a draft.'

So Kiera hands me a draft. I knew what my money was. Lisa had her own money, I was sending her *her* money and was sending her *my* money. I was giving her keep money, pay my house, pay her car. But I had my own separate money put into my own building society account and that was seven thousand pounds light.

I said to Kiera, 'Where's my £7,000 short?'

Kiera goes, 'It's between you and Lisa.'

When we were living in Northern Ireland, Lisa said that she wasn't happy with her figure and she wanted to get her breasts surgically enhanced. Dr Jan Stanick, the surgeon who performed the operation, had a clinic in Northern Ireland and he came over from Harley Street. I paid for it.

After a few years – I'm living in Birmingham at this stage – she wasn't happy with the size that she'd gone up to, and wanted to go even bigger. Big breasts seemed to be the fashionable thing!

This was at the very time I was going through different battles with the breweries, the protection racketeers, VAT, everything. I was trying to keep our heads above water. But all she seemed to care about was having her breasts even bigger. Nothing would suit her more.

So I paid for the second operation, the second enhancement. I can't remember when she actually had it done. At the time, I desperately needed the money for something else, but she wanted the operation, and for the sake of peace I gave in.

I'd bought the house in Kildare at this stage and I'd read about people in business going bankrupt and losing their property and I was a little bit naive thinking that they couldn't have taken the property in Ireland, so I'd put it in her name, thinking that we were going to be together for ever. All I could think about was that. I didn't want to be a failure in the business and lose my house because I'd worked my way up and I'd bought properties and made some money. And this was all I had.

I'd given Lisa everything she needed. The car she was driving – a Toyota Celica sports car. She was studying to be an accountant – I'd sent home computers, faxes, shredders, all stuff to set up an office in the house, so she'd be able to work from there. I'd been really looking after her.

I phoned her up again. Same thing again: 'Come near me and I'll have you arrested.'

On Wednesday, I went out jet skiing with my pals. On the Thursday, I woke up and I opened the newspaper and Lisa's sitting at the airport right next to Michael Flatley: 'FLATLEY'S NEW FRIEND'. So now I know there's another man involved, the world's biggest star.

This is my fiancée.

I went straight to her job. And, when they wouldn't open the door. Her boss said, 'No, go on away,' through the intercom system. So I bust open the door with my shoulder to show them no door can keep me out.

I went to her boss and I said, 'Shut your mouth. We're

not talking about a Mickey Mouse relationship; we're talking about a man's life, a house.'

So I went up to Lisa. And I looked at her – the eyes are the gateway to the soul. 'Tell me you're not with Flatley.' Because the newspaper had them sitting apart with arms folded.

She said, 'I went for the weekend down to his castle in Cork. He needed somebody to talk to. He's just come out of a relationship.'

'Well, tell him to phone the Samaritans if he needed somebody to talk to. You're my fiancée.' I was fuming. 'Where's my £7,000? What did he do, charge you to stay in his castle? Charge you to fly in his helicopter?'

She said, 'I love you, but I'm just not in love with you.'

I'm gutted, totally gutted. Out I go. There's no hate feeling at all for her. She was a nice girl. All right, she might have been money-motivated, she might have been wanting different things, but name me a woman that doesn't. She wasn't a good-time girl, but she was ambitious.

With hindsight, there's a lot of things I can now understand. When Lisa first met me, my fights had been on television in Ireland, and I was a big fish in a small pond. Suddenly, now my boxing career's finished, I wasn't the star any more, and she began to make comments about how I'd never get her into the *Hello!* magazine. At the time, I thought they were only jokes. But now, looking back, she obviously did want to be in *Hello!* magazine!

I drove to the airport on my own and flew back to Birmingham.

Now we used to have Irish dancing in the pub on a

Wednesday night in the function room. But this was a Thursday and we were having a raffle at the time. I've raised a lot of money for charities over the years and that particular time we'd raised £1,750 through the raffle for Acorns Hospice. So we were having the cheque presentation on the Thursday night, and I had to get back for that.

What I didn't realise was that one of the Irish dancers had won the raffle. So, rather than having the Irish dancing on a Wednesday and then having to come back on the Thursday for the cheque presentation, they'd changed the Irish dancing from a Wednesday to a Thursday. Meanwhile, everybody in England, everybody in my pub, would be aware of my relationship with Lisa and what was happening with Flatley now because it was in all the newspapers.

I drove back from the airport to my pub, and when I got there the Irish dancers, who normally dance in the function room, were all dancing round the lounge with the *River Dance* music playing. I took it personally, and thought they were all laughing at me. I stormed into my lounge. I was screaming and crying and I was shouting and fuming at everybody, 'You lousy bastards,' and everything, because I thought they were laughing at me, when they were only dancing for the presentation of the raffle.

My business partner is trying to calm me down. I was calling him names. I said, 'They're all laughing at me. It's bad enough what she did, they're all laughing.' I'm screaming and shouting, 'Fuck Flatley!' this that and everything.

The Irish newspapers were there to cover the cheque

presentation, but also to get my comments about Lisa and Flatley. None of them would normally have had much interest in the cheque presentation but because of what'd gone on with Flatley there were three Irish newspaper correspondents in the Midlands listening to 'I'm going to do this, I'm going to do that. Fuck Flatley!'

So now I'm arguing and screaming and shouting. And it all got blown out of proportion.

The next day, I've got Flatley's PR people on the phone. Chris Roach is dead now, God rest him. Chris said on the phone, 'Look, Michael Flatley wasn't aware that Lisa was with someone.' So she's denied me to Flatley!

But now he knows she's engaged. Any man with a shred of decency would back off until she and I had sorted out our differences. But no, he doesn't want to do that. On the contrary, knowing my record in the boxing, and because he'd once been a Golden Gloves boxing champion himself, his people see the opportunity for big publicity for his new tour. He's already had the *Lord of the Dance*, he's already had the *Riverdance*, now he's got his new one, the *Feet of Flames*. And he sees it as a perfect chance.

He gets pieces in the newspaper about me and him fighting over Lisa – with me getting knocked out! Egan and Flatley go to war over Lisa!

Two of my bar staff are on holiday in Turkey and Holland and they see it in the national newspapers in those countries because he's worldwide, Flatley, the Lord of the Dance.

Mike Tyson calls me and says he's read about it in a magazine in Las Vegas.

My illness now was getting worse; the court case was

still on, and I was as low as a man can go. It was a pretty bad time in my life, but I was determined not to lose.

Loads of times, I questioned God. I'm not a Holy Joe. I go to church and I say my prayers; I pray every night. You can ask any woman that's ever shared my bed at night before I go to sleep! I believe God made the world so everywhere is holy. A house is as good as a church if you're going to pray. You can pray anywhere.

And I've got friends that are priests and monks. When I eventually got sent to prison, for my character witness I had a priest, Father Thomas Malloy, my local parish priest at the Abbey Church, and the two nuns, Sister Helen Ward and Sister Josephine Walsh, were character witnesses for me. And Father David Connolly, a very personal friend, who's the priest at Willesden Green Prison, and our parish priest at home, Joe Drumgoole.

I've got friends in every religion and I respect every man's religion, no matter what God he prays to. I believe there's only one God, whatever name you want to call him. I call him God, some people call him Allah, some people call him Buddha. But whatever you want to call him, I still believe there's just the one God.

Anyway, the public-relations machine is making an even bigger issue of the business with Flatley.

Flatley was on Irish television and somebody asked him from the audience, 'Is it true you earn a million dollars a week?'

'No, I don't earn a million dollars a week, I earn a million *pounds* a week.'

How can you compete with a man like that for a

woman that seems interested in nothing other than that? My earning potential wasn't anywhere near his.

I'd put my house into her name because the pub was only a dream, but if the dream had succeeded I'd have a hundred houses and, if it didn't succeed, I didn't want to lose the one I'd got.

Now I'm concerned about the house. I said, 'I don't care about her any more, she's gone with Flatley. I can't change that. I'm not going to get her back, but I want my house. I want her to sign the house over.'

Chris Roach said, 'That's between you and Lisa. You sort that out with Lisa. Michael's only concerned about anything to do with him.'

But then he hinted that they'd get her to sign the house over if I was prepared to say that she and I had been finished months before, that she was a single woman.

So I said, 'I'll sign it. I want my house. I'll sign that we were finished months before.' So I'm going to keep him whiter than white. No problem.

Then they sickened the life clean out of me – they wanted me to sign that, even if me and him were to box, I would be no match for Michael Flatley. And that was the wreck of the deal. I freaked out, I went mad. I said, 'Fuck Flatley. He couldn't lace my gloves.'

TOMMY GIBBONS

During the time of the showdown in Dublin with Lisa, I was staying with my mum.

Normally I'm a private person and I don't like my mum knowing my personal problems because I don't want to upset her. But now I'm ranting and raving, and I'm on the phone to Lisa's mum, Irene, trying to find out exactly what's going on. She hangs up the phone on me. I'm fuming.

So my mum says, 'Who owes you £12,000?'

I say, 'Lisa's mum and dad.'

My mum rings Lisa's mum. She says, 'Whatever's going on between Joe and Lisa, that's their business. Give the boy his £12,000 back.'

Next thing, my mum receives in the post, from Lisa's family solicitor, a letter that you wouldn't send to a dog. It was a horrible letter saying that Mrs Egan is intimidating the Murphy family. What, a phone call asking for her son's money back?

My opinion was this solicitor has seen an opportunity. Now that Lisa is with Flatley, maybe he's got himself illusions that he is suddenly going to become Flatley's solicitor.

The letter really upsets my mum. She isn't too well with what was going on. She's had an aneurism, she's had a stress-related stroke. It's having a bad effect on her. All over the newspapers about her son's relationship with Lisa. Flatley's PR people making a big issue of it all. And now on top of everything having this solicitor's letter.

At this same time, I'm trying to get the house sorted out.

Tim Rocker, who's one of my closest friends, put me in touch with a personal friend of his called Tommy Gibbons, who's a solicitor within a small firm in Punchestown, Dublin.

Now Tommy is Tim's personal friend, Tim's my personal

friend, so Tommy is going to take an extra interest in this, not just from a solicitor's point of view, but also from a friendship point of view.

So it turns out that Lisa wants money to sign the house back over to me. So I have to pay money now to get my house back. It turns out that I've got to pay Lisa's solicitors and I've also got to pay my solicitor, plus a substantial amount of money to Lisa to take her name off the property.

I agree to pay the £2,700 to her solicitor and £2,000 to Tommy Gibbons. But, when we're going through the breakdown of Lisa's solicitor's bill, I find that I have to pay for a letter that the Murphy family have sent to my mother about the 'intimidating' phone call.

Now I'm boiling. It's already upset my mum, and now I'm paying for that upset. So I pay Tommy Gibbons his £2,000 and I said to him, 'Tommy, here's the £2,700 for Lisa's solicitor. A solicitor's word is as good as money in the bank. If you give me your word that that £2,700 is going to go across to Lisa's family solicitor, hold fire paying him. Whatever the deadline is, hold fire till the day before the deadline. And then pay him.'

£2,700 is a pittance to what solicitors earn, but I just wanted him to wait for his money because he was greedy in the fact that he was charging for that particular letter.

I said, 'Let him wait for the money.'

Tommy Gibbons says, 'I take my instructions off you, Joe.'

So the bill's sorted, Lisa's paid, the solicitor's paid, everything's set. All the cash sorted. I've gone back to England, starting to get my life in order again. I'd been very sick because of everything going on and I've got other battles coming up.

I've come into my pub this particular day and Madeleine, my barmaid, says, 'Joe, Tommy Gibbons the solicitor has been on the phone. He needs to talk to you about Flatley.'

My stomach's gone into knots because this is behind me now. I've gone into my office to make the phone call to Tommy thinking, 'What's happening now?' So I ring up Tommy Gibbons. I said, 'Tommy, I've got the message that you need to contact me about Flatley. What's happened?'

'Everything's cool, Joe,' he said, 'it's a dream come true.'

'Dream come true for who?'

He says, 'For me! It's like a *Rocky* story.'

I'm flummoxed. 'What do you mean a *Rocky* story?'

'Never in my wildest dreams did I ever think that I would have dealings with this particular firm of solicitors.'

'What firm of solicitors?'

'Flatley's solicitors.'

'What's Flatley's solicitors contacting you for?'

'No, it's all right. It's the money that you've given me to pay Lisa's family solicitor, the £2,700. I haven't paid him yet.'

'Why not?'

'Don't be worried, everything's OK. We're still within the deadline. You're OK.'

But obviously Lisa's family's been contacted by the solicitor to say that they haven't been paid the £2,700. This has been going on a long time. He says he wants his

£2,700. Lisa's family have contacted Lisa to say that the agreement was that the solicitor would get paid by me and I haven't paid. Lisa's obviously saying it to Flatley, and Flatley's getting a headache. So he's obviously instructed his solicitors in America, a huge firm, and their letter is faxed through to Tommy Gibbons to get this case closed: signed, sealed, over, pay the solicitor, so he can just put this to bed.

Tommy can't believe that he's had this correspondence. He's a solicitor in a small practice in Dublin. He's now getting contact from Michael Flatley's solicitors; he's now getting the deal with the champion of all the solicitors. Now suddenly he's with the big boys on the world scene of solicitors. He's got correspondence directed at him. And he is over the moon because these boys are not telling him, they're *asking* him to close this case.

In solicitor terminology, they can't dictate to him because he can drag it out. Is that what I'd like him to do?

I say, 'No, just put it to bed, Tommy. I've achieved what I wanted to achieve.'

CHAPTER EIGHT

Mike Tyson, My Friend

'I KNOW WHO BUNNY IS'

When Mike Tyson was over on the first trip to fight Julius Francis, I'd been speaking to Jay. Jay said, 'Joe I've got somebody here who wants to say hello to you.'

It's Mike. They've only just arrived. This is the first day they're here.

Mike says, 'Are you coming down to see me, Joe?'

So I say, 'I'll get down to see you when you're not in the gym.'

'I'm not in it on Sunday.'

'I'll be down soon.'

'Joe, please come down tomorrow.'

'I can't, Mike. I've got my business and everything else. But I will be coming down. Tuesday, I've a function on. I'll get down Wednesday.'

'No.'

'Yes, I'll get down Wednesday. I'm going to bring down some of my friends, guys that have stood with me on the doors during the trouble at my pub.'

'Joe, your friends are my friends.'

'I've got to bring Bunny Johnson down to see you. He's the former British heavyweight champion, the first black British heavyweight champion.'

Mike goes, 'I know who Bunny is and I know his achievements, Joe. It would be an honour to meet him.'

A quick story about Bunny. I put on the boxing tournament down in the pub. So I contacted the Irish Boxing Association. I've been a good ambassador for them, so I phoned them and said, 'I've got my pub, the function room. I want to put a boxing tournament on.'

'Oh, Joe, your venue's not big enough.'

'My function room's huge.'

Oh, they gave this excuse, that excuse.

I said, 'What's wrong with my function room? My business partner's an ex-Irish boxing champion; I'm an ex-Irish boxing champion. There's boxing teams coming over from Dublin all the time. I want to put a show on.'

'Well, it's not really prestigious enough.'

'What do you mean it's not really prestigious enough? Don't tell me it's not prestigious enough.' OK, it had a bad reputation. 'But I'm making it proper!'

Lo and behold anyway, there's a hotel just up the road from my pub. You've got to drive past my pub to get to the hotel. Now I'm an Irish boxing champion in the Midlands, there's a team coming over from Dublin and I don't even get an invite to the show. I hear about the show. They've gone past my front door to put a show on up the road! I've gone mad with the temper, fuming.

I ring up the Boxing Association again. The hatred runs deep. It's no good. I can't get a boxing tournament done in my pub.

So I went to a boxing show and I'm there with a friend of mine, Warren Wiggan, and a few of my lads. And I'm introduced to Bunny Johnson. He's the former British light heavyweight and heavyweight champion. He knocked out 'Dangerous' Danny McAlinden from Ireland, so I know Bunny's history.

I said, 'You won the Lonsdale Belt outright. It's an honour to meet you.'

He said, 'I know about the Lyndhurst. Tough pub.'

'My pub is a family pub. No tougher than any other pub. It's just on a housing estate that's pretty rough. It makes Beirut look like Beverly Hills. It's a rough estate. But there's good people on the estate and I've brought the community together. It'd be nice if you came to my pub. You might meet some friends there.'

'I'll leave this venue tonight.' Very dignified man. He said, 'I'll come to your pub tonight.'

I said, 'Oh that'll be great, that'll be great.'

Later, as we walked in the door of my pub, the first person he meets is my friend Cecil. They not only knew each other, but Cecil had been in Bunny's class in school, back in Jamaica! And they hugged and embraced. And I swear to God a choreographer couldn't have put it together better.

I said, 'I told you, you'll meet an old school friend.'

So he says, 'There's a warmth here. You're right. It is a family pub.'

When I told him the story about the Irish Boxing Association, he said, 'I'll put a boxing tournament on.'

And I said, 'Yeah, OK, no problem.' I just thought it was talk.

The next day, he was back up. He said, 'I've made my phone calls. I've got St Theresa's Boxing Club in Handsworth. We can put a tournament together.'

And we put two boxing tournaments on. So me and him had become very good friends.

So, as soon as the call with Mike Tyson finished, I phoned up Bunny.

'Hey, Joe.'

'Mike Tyson can't wait to meet you.'

'Don't tell lies.'

'Bunny, I don't tell lies. I've just come off the phone to him and he said he can't wait to meet you.'

There was nine of us on the first trip to see Mike. Over a period of four days, I brought everybody down. I had 24 friends down. The last day I took Danny Brown, John McBean, Jim, my barman, Daniel Heggarty, my barman, and Martin Murrall, my girlfriend Ruth's cousin.

On the first day when we went down, Mike Tyson walked over to Bunny Johnson and he bows his head. 'Mr Johnson, sir.'

Bunny couldn't believe it.

Mike said, 'It's an honour to meet you.'

Bunny was in shock because Mike Tyson was in awe of

meeting Bunny Johnson. And it was lovely to see, because Bunny Johnson's a very humble man.

Then Mike said, 'You went into Rahway State Penitentiary, New Jersey. You fought Jim Scott there.' Jim Scott did a lot of armed robberies. Fought a load of pro fights.

And Bunny said, 'That's right, yeah.'

Mike said, 'When I was 12 years old, I watched that fight on television. While I was in prison, Jim Scott wrote to me, "Keep your chin up, Mike, everything will be OK." At the end he wrote, "PS Mike, keep doing your push-ups."' Mike was able to tell Bunny that Jim Scott had just been released, after 29 years in prison.

And he said to Bunny, 'You were No. 2 in the world behind Muhammad Ali.'

And Bunny went, 'That's right, yeah.'

And I was looking at them. I said, 'You were No. 2 in the world?'

I knew he'd been the British heavyweight champion, and then went down and won the light heavyweight title, then he won the Lonsdale Belt outright, and he was also the Commonwealth champion. And he's been a great ambassador for British boxing, a great ambassador for the black community; he's just a normal great guy. But I never knew he was once rated No. 2 in the world. He was some fighter.

Then Mike turns to me, and he says, quiet like, 'Hey, Joe.' We hadn't seen each other for years.

Mike was staying at the Grosvenor Hotel. He knew the history of the Grosvenor and that's why he wanted to stay there, because he's a historian of boxing, and he's so knowledgeable about boxing. The Grosvenor Hotel is part of the history of British boxing. Bunny actually won one of his titles there.

Mike Tyson was in awe of Bunny Johnson. He was also in awe of Alan Minter and he wanted to meet Alan Minter more than he wanted to meet any other fighter in England. And he said, 'Please get Alan Minter to come and see me here in the hotel.'

Alan was also Britain's last undisputed world middleweight champion. He's a character, a genuine nice guy, and so down to earth. And he was also my friend.

So, when we were in the hotel, I contacted Alan and he came down. And Mike Tyson is getting to meet somebody that he obviously idolises, Alan Minter! And the two of them just chatted.

'NOBODY PUTS THEIR HAND ON JOE!'

The first day we were there, there's a couple of his security, guys standing there with these big muscles. And Mike's pulling me, 'Hey, Joe, my brother.' And next moment I've turned around and none of my friends are following me.

I said, 'Where's my friends?'

Mike said, 'Where's Joe's friends?'

His security have stopped all my friends coming down.

'Let Joe's friends through!'

I said, 'That's my friend, he's my friend.'

The guy looks at me, and he goes, 'You've got a lot of friends.'

I said, 'Yes. And Mike Tyson's my friend too.'

Later on that day, one of my pal's punching the bag. This same muscular security guard comes over. He knows who are my friends now. 'Don't be punching the bag; you might damage the bag.'

So my friend says, 'If Mike Tyson can't damage the bag, there's no chance of me damaging the bag.'

The next day, I'm down at the gym with another group of friends. This same guy's there. He's not making my friends welcome. Mike's making all my friends welcome. But this one muscular security guard isn't.

The next day he's bothering somebody else.

The fourth day, the world's press is there, so the gym is like a sauna and I'm soaking with sweat. Mike had been coming out for dinner with us the previous days to the Hard Rock Café, but this particular day he couldn't come out with us because he had to return to the world's press to give interviews and stuff. So he said, 'I won't be able to go out with you afterwards, Joe, but you're going out for some food with Jay.' That's Jay Bright, his stepbrother and his friend.

So I said, 'Yeah.'

And there's all the entourage and the press and we're out in the hall now at this stage and my shirt's wringing with sweat from the heat of the gym. And he said, 'You'd better change your shirt.'

'No, I'm OK.'

'You can't go out like that, Joe, you'll catch a cold. Have you anything else to wear?'

'No, I'm OK, Mike.'

'Hang on.'

One of the guys was carrying his sports bag, and he reached in and took out a brand-new Everlast T-shirt. He said, 'Here, put that on.'

So I took my shirt off.

He said, 'Go into the bathroom, Joe, and change your shirt.'

So I went into one of the toilets. Now he's holding up the whole movement of the entourage, everybody; the world's press now have stopped for me to change my shirt!

And I went into the bathroom and, when I came out, I've got this Everlast shirt on. And I say, 'Are you happy now?'

He said, 'I'm happy now.'

And then I put my damp shirt back on over it.

He said, 'What are you doing?'

'I'm all right, Mike.'

He covers his face with his hands in disbelief.

I said, 'I'm OK.'

So now the entourage is moving on. I look down to button my shirt up and, as I looked down to button my shirt up, this same muscular bodyguard that's been bothering my friends pushes me back.

Now I took my eyes off him, so I'm knocked off balance as he launches me back. Quick as I'm launched back, I'm back up again. But, as quick as I'm back up again, Mike has pushed through my barman, Daniel Brown, to get to this minder.

And Anthony, one of his two main minders from America – Cornelius is the other one – jumps in now because Mike's at this English minder that's pushed me. Anthony jumps in and he grabs Mike's hand. And he says, 'All right, Mike, I've got it.'

And the veins, I swear to God, the veins were coming out of Mike's neck. 'Nobody puts their hand on Joe. Joe's my personal friend. Nobody touches Joe, nobody!

I say, 'Mike, Mike, it's OK.'

'No, Joe, nobody touches you, nobody.'

'It's all right, Mike, it's all right.'

Anthony goes, 'It's OK, Joe. Mike, calm down. It's OK. Joe, it's OK. Take this man out of here.'

This muscular bodyguard now has shrunk like this. He's ushered away.

And Mike says, 'Are you all right?'

'I'm OK, Mike, I'm OK.'

We went to the meal in the Hard Rock and Jay was explaining to Daniel. And he said, 'You don't understand Joe's relationship with Mike. The love, the friendship. It's hard to put into words.'

I've never sold him out. I've never done any wrong to him. We go back over 20 years.

He says, 'Joe has a special relationship with Mike. Mike takes it personal. Anyone puts their hand on Joe, he takes it very personal.'

We went back up to Birmingham that night. We're in my pub. I get a phone call from Jay. He says, 'Joe, Mike wants to speak to you for a minute.'

So Mike comes on the phone. He's done all his work, world's press conference, everything else. He says, 'Are you OK, Joe?'

'Yeah, I'm sound, Mike.'

'I'm sorry my man pushed you.'

'No, it's all right, Mike.'

'Can I speak to Daniel, your barman.'

'Yeah, OK.' I went out. I said, 'Daniel, Mike Tyson wants to speak to you on the phone.'

He said, 'What?'

'Mike Tyson wants to speak to you on the phone, Daniel, come into my office.' A couple of people followed him in.

I heard Mike's voice on the phone. 'Daniel, I'm sorry that I had to push you, but that guy pushed Joe and I had to get to him. Are you OK?'

And Daniel goes, 'Yeah, I'm OK. I'm all right.'

'Please accept my apologies.'

'Yeah, it's sound, no problem.'

Later, Danny said to me, 'I can't believe it, Mike Tyson is concerned about *me*!'

I said, 'That's how dignified he is.'

People don't see that side of Mike Tyson, that's how dignified and how lovely the man is. He was concerned for my barman and my friend, Daniel, who he'd had to push out of the way to get to this minder that had pushed me.

YOUR FRIENDS ARE MY FRIENDS

Mike knew that I'd been shot. We've spoken a number of times about it and he knows about what happened; he knows about the men that stood beside me, the courage of the men that stood beside me for no financial gain, just friendship.

When I brought these men down to meet Mike in the hotel, Mike said to me in front of all my friends, 'Joe, your friends are my friends.' It made me feel so proud.

He had his giant minders around him, Cornelius, who's a powerful big black man, and Anthony who's another powerful black man, and Steven Fitch, 'Crocodile', the cheerleader-cum-minder, a bit loud, in the crocodile-khaki gear.

Then Mike said, 'Joe, any more trouble at your pub and *I'm* landing.'

One of the giant minders went, 'Right on, Mike!'

And Mike looked at him, like, I don't need you. I got Joe's friends. Because he knew that these men had put their life on the line for me for no financial gain. He's got two minders here that are probably on half a million a year, and wouldn't do what these men had done for me, for nothing.

GOLD TEETH

I've got a photograph of Mike, signing a poster to a friend of mine, Nigel Rafferty. He had 104 professional fights.

He's got gold teeth. And I told Mike, 'Mike, Nigel's got gold teeth like you.'

And Mike is signing the poster of Nigel, smiling, showing the gold teeth.

The night of the Birmingham bomb scare, we were at a Ron Grey function, the Summer Ball. It's come over the news about Birmingham bombs going off in the city centre, people leaving, soldiers on the streets. And suddenly there's a sombre atmosphere.

One table beside us, eight people left and, on the other table beside us, all 10 people left, and there was ones and twos everywhere. So the mood was pretty solemn.

My mum rang me. I said, 'Mum, I'm not in Birmingham, I'm in Dudley.'

'Oh, thank God,' she says.

I thought, 'What am I going to do here?' Ron Grey's the boxing promoter, there's a number of boxers in the hall with their families, a great group. Now the mood's gone because people are concerned about their families in Birmingham.

So I rang Mike.

I said, 'Hello, Mike, it's Joe in England.'

'Hey, Joe, how are you doing?'

'Mike, there's some bombs going off in Birmingham.'

'Are you OK?'

'I'm not in Birmingham, Mike, I'm in Dudley.'

'Oh great, Joe.'

'But I'm at a function and the mood's pretty sombre. Can I put you on to a few people to say hello just to cheer them up?'

'Yeah, by all means.'

'The first guy I'm going to put you on to is Nigel Rafferty, my friend you signed the poster for, 104 fights.'

He gets on to the phone with Mike. 'Yeah, Nigel, we're going to have to compare gold teeth.' Now for him to be able to remember that.

I put him on to the phone with another person, then more people, one after the other. The atmosphere started buzzing again.

The phone bill came to something horrific that month, but I didn't care. At that moment, Mike Tyson was lifting everybody's spirits.

It was something very special.

My old friend Stuart was there, with his brother Simon. Stuart is a chartered accountant and his brother Simon has a cigarette vending-machine company, Global Vending; he used to fill my cigarette machines up. I've known them both for a number of years.

I put Stuart on to him – he couldn't believe it. He said, 'I'm talking to Mike Tyson.'

And everybody – even some of the old pros were there speaking to Mike – could not believe it. Mike Tyson spoke to them all, 20 to 25 people.

'Hi, enjoy your meal, don't worry about your families, everything will be OK.'

It was just wonderful. It showed the lovely man he is.

NO RADIO? NO THANKS!

Mike has a fascination with cars. He had at one time an amazing collection of fantastic cars. When he was down in London at the Grosvenor House Hotel, we went along with him to the shop on Park Lane, the Mclaren shop, to look at this particular car, the Mclaren F1, something like that. It's the fastest road car in the world. We went in and, as it's a million-pound car, if you were a potential buyer of this car, you were going to be shown the utmost hospitality. If Joe Bloggs comes in off the street and he hasn't got any way of buying this car, he probably wouldn't get the same hospitality, but they knew Mike had the finances to buy this car. So he was given the red-carpet treatment. So he's looking at this car, he's like a child with the car, he's fascinated with it. Anyway, I'm looking, and it's a bucket seat. There's only one seat in the car, set in the middle. It's a Formula 1 sports car. They showed us the engine at the back, and it's just unbelievable. Anyway, Mike was well impressed with the car; the performance of the car was second to none.

Everything was fantastic. And Mike was almost going to buy the car. And then he said, 'Where's the music system?'

And they said, 'No, there's no music system in this car. There's no way you could put a music system into this car.'

And Mike said, 'No, I don't want the car, it hasn't got a music system in the car.'

The people in the Mclaren shop couldn't believe it.

Mike loves his music.

VALUE FOR MONEY

We were Mike Tyson's guests at the fight with Kevin McBride, and Showtime had brought us over. I've got photographs in the car of Muhammad Ali, my dad, and me and my girlfriend Ruth (more of whom later). We went to Washington DC on the Friday, and the fight was on the Saturday.

On the Friday night, Showtime were bringing us out for a meal to a restaurant. So I'm staying with Ruth, they've checked us into the hotel where all the British and Irish press are staying, and where the press conference for the fight was. Beautiful hotel.

And I said to Ruth, 'Go on, get yourself ready, come

on, hurry up! Hurry up, Ruth, they're not bringing us to the Ritz!'

Where did they bring us? She said, 'Not bringing us to the Ritz? Look where they're bringing us to!'

When we get to the Ritz, all the Showtime people are there, and they bring out a beautiful meal. On the Saturday, we've got the VIP press passes, and we're sitting in the VIP section. Me and my dad are brought out to the changing rooms to see Mike, as he's requested us to come out. I'd been with Tom Patti the day before and some of the Showtime people, Tom Casino and Ivy. But, on the night of the fight, Mike's requested me and my dad to come to the changing rooms.

So we get there, big hug. Mike's calm as you like, cool and calm. I've got a photograph of him signing a little pink boxing glove for my niece.

Mike said, 'Joe, tell us some stories.' And it was lovely.

'Mike, you're getting ready for the fight.'

'No, tell us some stories.'

'After the fight.'

Patti and I chatted. I said to him, 'Look we're friends over 20 years! We haven't done bad.'

It was really, really nice.

Mike had spoken to my dad over the phone, but he'd never met him. And it was lovely. Geoff Fenwick who was training Mike was there. And it was a lovely atmosphere in the changing rooms.

Now I wouldn't go down and see Mike and not go in and see Kevin, because I've known Kevin for a number of years. So I walked across to Kevin's changing room. Went in, and got a lovely reception. Kevin was lying on the ground getting exercises to his legs.

I said, 'Kevin, I won't shake hands because you're exercising.'

'Joe, good to see you.'

'The very best of luck. I've just been in to see Mike. The very best of luck.'

'Great, Joe.'

So we left, and we went back to ringside and to our seats. Mike signed a few bits and pieces for us when we were in the changing rooms, lovely posters for the family. It was just before the fight, but he was lovely and calm.

In the fight Mike was beaten. He'd hit Kevin with some of his best shots but the desire wasn't there any more. He'd hit Kevin with his best punches and Kevin was still standing.

After the fight we were at the press conference – we were in the VIP seats for the fight and we were brought out to the press conference with the press passes. So there's me, my dad and Ruth sitting there. All the British and the world's press are there. And Pascal Collins was on the stage with Kevin.

And Kevin said, 'I would like to thank Joe Egan and his family for coming over,' which was a lovely gesture, for Kevin McBride to say that at the press conference.

Then Mike was brought in. And Mike said, 'I would like to thank Joe Egan and his family for coming over.' And it was lovely.

And next Mike said, 'Joe, you were there at the beginning, and you're there at the end.'

And one of the British press or one of the American press said, 'Mike, do you think you gave the fans value for money tonight?'

Now we're there with the press passes, but we shouldn't really be at the press conference; it's only because of the friendship with Mike.

Well, like a lot of Irishmen, my dad is a bit highly strung. Next thing, my dad stands up and says, 'What are you on about, value for money? He's given the fans 20 fucking years of value for money!'

I'm saying, 'Sit down, Dad.'

Everybody starts cheering and clapping.

And Mike goes, 'Thank you, Mr Egan.' So dignified.

My dad's going on, 'Twenty fucking years of value for money.'

'Dad, all right, Dad, sit down, Dad.'

But what a stupid comment for a man to make: 'Do you think you gave the fans value for money tonight, Mike?' That man shadow boxing is value for money. He put heavyweight boxing back on the map when it was in the doldrums.

And now at the press conference after the defeat, he was so dignified, it was beautiful. He said, 'Boxing has only been one chapter in my life. My wife is rich and my children are rich. What more could a man want?'

CHAPTER NINE

Hard Times

RUTH

Well, when I came over to this country first with Paddy Finn, Paddy had a man working for him, Noel Delaney, he's since dead now, God rest him. Now I'd worked in Dublin Airport with Noel's brother, Eamon Delaney, without realising they were brothers. I knew Noel when I come over, as I was introduced to him. So when I eventually came over to live in Birmingham, me and Noel became close friends and it turned out that I knew his brother.

When I moved from the Dubliner and come over to the Lyndhurst, I still was only two years in the pub trade, and I still wasn't the most knowledgeable to run a big pub. But I had ambition and enthusiasm and I had confidence that I could do it. I also had the backing of my business partner, Tom, so we'd got the money, we'd got the muscle and we'd got the enthusiasm. But Noely was very, very knowledgeable in the running of pubs because he'd been in the pub trade so many years. He knew the ins and outs of the trade. So Paddy, fair play to him, allowed Noely to come over and work with us in the Lyndhurst as well as the Dubliner. And Noely used to come from Acocks Green, work in the Dubliner and then come over to the Lyndhurst. And Noely and myself became great friends. He was the hardest-working man I've ever seen. I've never seen a man could work as hard as that man. Unbelievable. One day, his son Sean took his car and Noely cycled from Acocks Green over to Erdington. It's a good cycle. In his late sixties, and he cycled over not to let me down, to come over and work in the pub. Just an unbelievable man.

And it was through Noely that I met his brother John. John and Sheila are Ruth's mum and dad, and Ruth is Noel's niece. So now I meet John, who's Eamon and Noely's brother.

I hadn't met Ruth yet!

It was funny when we met John. Me and Noely were after going down to get change in the Post Office and we met John there. Even though they were brothers and he only lived round the corner from the pub, Noel had never spoken to me about John. Noel used to come over to the pub, very efficient, hard working, and just get on with his work. He was my friend, one of my closest friends, but he never spoke about his personal life – so next thing I'm introduced to his brother. I said, 'Well, come up to the pub, use the pub.'

So John came up with his wife Sheila and I became great

friends with John and Sheila, and it was through them that Ruth came up to the pub. She came up one afternoon.

Ruth was working in Erdington in the Halifax. The pub had a particularly bad reputation when we took it over, but we were cleaning it up. And Ruth had heard her mum and dad talking about myself and she was looking forward to meeting me. My relationship with Lisa was over at this stage. And to start with there was nothing like that between me and Ruth, we were just friends and our families were friends.

One day I just asked her out. We went for a meal and stuff. And suddenly I'm courting her!

But, at that particular time, I had all the battles with the brewery and everything else and I wasn't too well. And, fair play to her, she helped with everything, because I took very, very sick as a result of everything that happened.

My youngest brother had come over to help us in the pub at different times to give us his knowledge of the trade as well and to help me. And Connolly, my youngest brother, is a very good-looking boy, and I actually thought that Ruth fancied Connolly. And we joke and I still tease her about that to this day.

DESPERATION

The pub, the battle, the court battle, the relationship battle – everything was just coming on top. I had very, very low self-esteem, everything was just getting too much. And then I thought I was going to lose my house in Ireland that was in Lisa's name, so I was trying to hold on to the house; and I was living in England because the brewery were trying to evict me. It was just getting too much. And then it was costing me a fortune in legal fees, with a solicitor in Ireland fighting the battle with Lisa, and a solicitor in England fighting the battle with the brewery. So I was paying out any money I was making and any money that I'd saved in legal fees.

There was a barman in the pub called John O'Sullivan. He was from Cork but he'd been married to a Dublin girl called Kelsh, whose brother Patrick I knew. John had broken up his relationship in Dublin and had come to Birmingham to work for me. One day, his sister came into the pub with her boyfriend who was a car dealer, a guy called Robin Weaver. He offered me an opportunity to do some business with him. Let him conduct his business in the pub and park his cars in the car park of me and my business partner's pub.

So I thought, 'Well, it'd be an extra income if he spends his money in the pub and the people he's doing business with will be spending their money in the pub.' I tried to encourage as much business into the pub as I possibly could.

Then he said he was doing hooky cars, and would I mind him parking hooky cars on the car park, and he would throw me some extra money. Well, at that particular time, I was at a very low ebb. I was also in a very bad financial state because I was paying all these solicitors out, and I was working 18 hours a day, 19 to 20 hours a day some days.

I was the first up in the morning, I was the last to go to bed at night, and I was the last to get paid. And I was paying all this money out in legal fees, which I deeply begrudged paying.

Now this opportunity had come up to do something I'd never done before in my life.

When my back was to the wall a number of times, I'd always made ends meet. But at this moment I was very bitter, I was very sick, I was very twisted and I was very confused. And I decided to do a quick crime so I could use the money to pay legal fees, to pay Lisa coming out the house. Because I thought what she was doing to me was a bigger crime, making me pay for a house that she hadn't paid for, so my money's been paying for the house twice.

So I've gone and got involved in stolen cars.

GREED

At the time I thought, 'Well, it's easy money,' and at the time I was begrudging working hard to pay legal fees. So I thought, 'Well, it's a crime what's been done to me, I'll use criminal money to pay that off.' My intentions were just to pay the £19,700 – the £15,000 to Lisa, £2,700 to her solicitor and the £2,000 to my solicitor. So all I wanted to do was to get that £19,700. Anyway, after getting the £19,700 pretty easy – to tell you the truth, the cars were flying in and flying out – I suddenly realised I'm breaking my heart working in the pub for 16 to 17 hours a day and I've got this £19,700 in a matter of weeks, in a couple of months. And then the greed kicked in.

I've never been greedy in my life, but, until it actually happens to you, you can't explain. It just takes control. I'd got this £19,700 that had come so easy to me. My fortune was somebody else's misfortune and I regret it to this day and I'll probably regret to my dying day what I actually did because I'd had a car stolen off me once, and it's something that you work hard for for somebody else to take, or for somebody else to damage. It's not nice, so for me to suddenly be involved with people taking other people's belongings, it's something I've got to live with.

And it was greed. I don't drink alcohol, I don't take drugs, I like to have full control of what I do. So at that moment in time I had full control of what I was doing. But the greed was controlling me.

I couldn't stop because of greed. It's easy money.

And I regret ever doing it, I've paid my debt to society, I've done my time. It's not nice. It's one of the seven deadly sins, and for somebody that has got great willpower and great determination, great strength of character like me to give in so easy. That's it.

It's deadly. And it just takes over. And it's horrible.

FEAR

Seven months before, the guy that had shot me and the old man had gone missing for months. People had scoured everywhere looking for him but he'd gone off the face of the planet. Now he walked up and handed himself in at a police station. Five people went to identify him for doing the shooting because he'd no mask. He walked free after 36 hours.

A female police sergeant phoned me from Sutton Coldfield Court. She said, 'Joe, I've bad news for you. The courts won't let us hold Jake Welch for more than

36 hours. We're going to have to release him. He's back. Be careful.'

I said, 'Thank you for your advice, sergeant.'

That very week, on the Sunday, the pub was busy. My 14-year-old nephew, my sister's boy, had come over from America and I'd gone out for a meal with him. When I got back, one of my barmaids was panicking.

'Oh, Jesus Christ, we've a fellow on the phone, he's saying, "I'm going to kill everybody, shoot everybody."'

I said, 'Look, it's all right. If I had a pound for everyone that was going to shoot me, I'd be a rich man. It's only talk.'

The phone rings again. I pick up the phone. It's Jake Welch.

Now he's the one that's already shot me, so it's not a man that's making idle threats. But now I don't want to show any weakness.

He said, 'I'm going to shoot you, I'm going to blow the bollocks out of you. I'm going to blast the brains out of your skull.'

'Yeah, OK, OK, bring it on,' I said. 'Don't talk about it, just do it. If you want to do it, come on, bring it on.'

Ruth has picked up the extension in the bar and she's listening to this. When we hang up, she's panicking.

I'm saying, 'It's all right, Ruth, calm down, don't worry.

So I've now got my 14-year-old nephew and Ruth and me frightened, and it's a fear like I've never gone through before. I've been afraid before, but now I'm afraid for them, whereas before I've just been afraid for myself.

It was a fear I couldn't handle, plus I was weakened, I was sick. I didn't know what to do.

The police had come to the pub because they'd been called by the barmaid. She made a statement to them. Then they asked me to make a formal statement.

I said, 'Five people have made statements against this guy before. He walked free after 36 hours. Five people went to identify him. He walked free. I'd state the fact that he's a grass. He's working hand in cuff with you, so I'm not going to make a statement against him.'

That was on the Sunday evening.

On the Tuesday morning, in the early hours, Bosh! Straight through the doors. The full armed police.

I'm in bed. They've come up the stairs, all boiler-suited up with their machine guns and everything else, they're screaming and they're shouting. It was frightening.

My nephew's up. So they're searching everywhere upstairs. A search warrant for car documents, but they were really looking for something else.

My dogs are going mad on the roof. My nephew says, 'Can I take the dogs down?'

I repeated what they said: 'Nobody leaves until they leave.'

My cleaning staff arrive to clean the pub. They've got them sitting downstairs, as they're searching downstairs now. They close the door on the office. They come up to call me out. Now don't forget they've got us sitting. Everywhere they went and searched, we were in their presence, upstairs, with them, every room they searched. Downstairs they've got me sitting with two CID officers in the lounge. Two of my cleaners, and now my barmaids have arrived.

Next of all, at the back I could hear them screaming

and shouting. They bring me out and they produce a gun. They say, 'What's that?'

'A handgun.'

'What are these?'

'Bullets.'

'What's the gun doing under your roof?'

'It's a set-up.' They hadn't found it in my presence. They know they've fucked up. 'Look, that gun's found at the back. The delivery staff, everybody, now has access to that area.'

So they give me bail. But now I've rubbed them up the wrong way. They're really determined to get me now. They had a fair idea there were hooky cars being done. It didn't warrant surveillance. But, because they've fucked up on the gun, it's now personal. And I'm warned by my retired senior police officer that they're out to get me.

They've put every sort of surveillance cameras on top of the flats. They produced photographs of me in cars. They put me under surveillance for months.

Eventually, they capture a guy who was delivering two cars to Ireland. He was driving one, a BMW, and another fellow was driving the other, a Jeep. Instead of going straight to the boat at Holyhead, the BMW guy's took a diversion to go and see a barmaid who used to work with me up in Wales that I had to let go because she was a bit too promiscuous, which was causing problems! She was seeing a couple of customers and causing problems with their marriages and everything else, so I had to let her go.

He was thinking that the guy in the Shogun Jeep was going to take two hours to get to the boat, when he could do it in an hour, so he could divert and see this girl for an hour, and get back to catch the Holyhead ferry to Dublin.

So he's spotted speeding in this 850 BMW, the registration was B1WOW because the car was a wow. He takes the chase; they put the stingers down. He goes into the ditch.

Instead of coming out and saying that it was *his* stolen car, he tells the whole operation. Now not only do they have photographs of me getting in and out of cars that were hooky, but they've also got a grass.

But of course I didn't know about this.

They've hit my business partner at his house and arrested him. They've got me, and they've arrested my brother, who had nothing to do with anything.

Then they offered us a deal.

You know when you're a kid and you're in a fight and you get somebody in a headlock and the guy goes, 'I'll give you the draw.' You know they'll give you the draw because you've got the win.

So, when the police offered us a deal, I said to Tommy, 'No, don't take any deal. It's like the draw when we were kids. I'm not going to take the draw, I've got the win.' It was a stupid childish mentality.

He said, 'Take the deal.'

'I'm not taking any deal.'

So Tommy, my best friend, said, 'I'll go with you, Joe, but I think we should take the deal.' If I'd fought it and I hadn't won, and he'd taken the deal he'd have felt bad. So he went with me.

And lo and behold, they produced the grass in court.

They've produced photographic evidence of me getting in and out of various cars. And it was too late to take the deal.

I'd had to sell my own car – a BMW 525 turbo diesel – to pay legal fees. I sold my Jeep to pay legal fees for the battles with Lisa and with the brewery. At the time when the police hit us, I had to use a borrowed Rover Metro to go up and down to the bank because I'd sold everything that I had to pay legal fees. That's how low I was. I'd sold everything. I'd sold my 18th birthday watch and I'd sold my 21st birthday ring.

I remember the only time I'd ever seen my dad cry, we were too young to understand. We came home one day and my mum was agitating and panicked. We were only kids, and I didn't realise what was wrong. It turned out that my granddad had died, my dad's dad. We'd only met him a couple of times. I didn't really know him that well. But he was still my granddad, he was still my daddy's dad. And me and my brother were a bit panicking ourselves because my mum was agitated, she was running around like a headless chicken. My dad came in from work and she said he'd better phone home. So me and my brother were sitting on the stairs and we heard my dad making the phone call. In every boy's eyes, his dad is the toughest man in the world. I remember watching my dad cry at the bottom of the stairs on the phone. I'd never felt fear like it. I was terrified because, now my dad's crying, I didn't know what was going on. And I found out that his daddy had died, God rest him.

When I was found 'Guilty' in court, I looked up into the

balcony, and I saw my dad crying. It was eerie, like, you know – but the only time I'd seen him cry before was when his dad had died. So me getting sent to prison had the same effect on my dad as his dad dying. I felt sick, sick as a man could feel.

This was when I was found 'Guilty', before any sentencing. I was remanded straight away and sent downstairs. The security guys were around me in the dock because I suppose for the prisoners jumping the dock and stuff like that. But before I went down the stairs, down to the basement, I'd seen my dad and Ruth crying.

Warwick Crown Court. We were brought back and, a couple of days or a week later, you get sentenced. Judge Coates was quite lenient with the sentencing because of my previous good record. He gave us two and a half years but the police weren't happy and appealed, and the Crown Prosecution got us four years. They never appealed against my brother, but they appealed against me and my business partner because we'd upset them by proving them wrong before. I was gutted for my business partner, and because my brother was innocent.

My brother had only come over to help me during my illness and now they'd got him. He got two years and he did a year in prison. His missus was Canadian and she met my brother when she was over on holiday from Canada. They fell in love and had a baby, but he missed the birth of his child. He's since sold his house in Northern Ireland and gone to Canada. He hadn't been involved in anything. All he'd done was come over and help me run my pub while I was sick.

CATEGORY B

When we went for the final day of the court battle, I said to my business partner, Thomas McGeough, 'Tom, you know we're going in for the last day now. It's not looking great, but we've got to go in as if we're still going to win.'

So Tom said, 'No, I'm going to wear my tracksuit in, because, if I'm found Guilty, I want to be able to go to prison in a tracksuit. At least I can be comfortable in my tracksuit.'

'Tom, if you go in in a tracksuit, it looks like you're throwing the towel in. Let's go in in a nice suit, a shirt and tie, and show that we still feel that we're innocent men and that we can walk out in our nice suits. But don't take it for granted that we're going to prison.'

So Tom, who'd been experienced in court battles and had done prison time before, I talked him out of going into court in his tracksuit. So, on the final day, we're found 'Guilty'. We were remanded straight away, and we were brought down.

I've gone down the stairs and Tom was saying, 'What am I doing in a suit?' And he's turned around to me and he pointed at me. 'You told me to come in a suit. What am I doing in a suit?' And he trips and he pulls the sole of his shoe off.

So I'm laughing to myself going down the stairs and he's walking along now and his shoe's flapping. So, when they brought us from the courtroom to the prison, he's walking along with this flapping shoe. Even though I was churning inside, it gave me a little giggle inside about his flapping shoe.

We were originally sent to Blakenhurst Prison, which was a 23-hour-a-day lock-up. You had an hour a day out of your cell. It was classed as a Category B prison.

When you get there, they bring you to reception. They take off your suits and stuff and they put them into a box. You sign for what you're putting in. If you've a watch or anything on, sometimes they let you keep it, depending on the value. For insurance, they only allow you to keep things of a certain value. Anyway, I had a nice watch. They took it, saying it was an expensive watch. The senior officer informs you of the rules, exactly what's going on.

They take all your clothes, and they give you a prison uniform, jeans and a prison shirt. They gave us prison sneakers. They call them prison sneakers, with just two stripes, because Adidas had the three stripes. They were just like plimsolls, like a flat plimsoll, and they hadn't any laces in them. That's what we had to wear. And they hadn't got a shirt to fit me, so I'm like a deformed man in this shirt. They wouldn't let us wear our own shirt, our own clothes, so I've got this shirt that's about three sizes too small, a pair of jeans that were skin tight and a pair of slip-on plimsolls with no laces, so all the other prisoners know you're new lads in and they're looking at us.

Tom got a single cell. My brother and I got a cell together, which, to my surprise, was pretty clean. The prison was clean because it was reasonably new. I was surprised because you hear about all these prison stories, the conditions that they've got in prison. So it was much cleaner than I expected. But it still wasn't very nice. And, years before, I used to watch *Porridge*, and you'd hear the gates of Slade Prison on the television slamming behind you. But, until you actually hear that cell door slamming and the key locking, you don't realise, it's a nightmare. The first job we got was on the prison servery, so we could get out of our cell a little bit more than the average prisoner because we had to go down to do the servery for breakfast, lunch and evening meal. So we went down, we cleaned the servery, and we'd meet other prisoners that were working on the servery as well. So it would give you a little bit more freedom – just to get out of your cell for that little bit extra, whereas, apart from the half-hour that they would have to walk the square outside, the other prisoners would be in their cell all day, they'd come down to get their meal on their tray and bring it back up to their cell.

I heard that they used to eat together in the same canteen but then there was a bit of friction, a bit of trouble, and the prison officers couldn't control all the prisoners in one canteen. So now the different house blocks would come down in turn, get their food on to their tray and straight back up to their cell. So you ate in your cell.

I was on house block 6. So from house block 6 you had to go through all the five house blocks. So we'd leave the servery. The prison officer would open the gate out of the servery, then lock the gate. We'd go down to the next house block. Open the gate, put us through, lock the gate. So we did this nearly every day. So not only was I getting my cell door locking behind me, but I'd also hear all these cell doors and all these gates locking. And it's not a nice sound, to know that you're behind a steel door. It's not a nice feeling to hear it locking and it's not a nice feeling to know that you're in there. I wouldn't recommend it to anybody. It's very degrading what you're got to go through in the prison. I'm not saying they made you feel like an animal, but you do.

Most of the time, except for the hour that you were out, you were locked up. In the morning, your cell would be opened and you'd have 20 minutes to maybe go and get yourself showered before you go down and get your breakfast. Then back into your cell, locked till mid-morning, till you get your lunch.

My brother Connolly had nothing to do with the crime, genuinely had nothing to do with it. The boy had come over to help me in my pub; he'd trained as a barman in Ireland and he'd come over to help me.

He's a little bit fragile at the best of times because, when my family were evicted in 1986, Connolly was there at the time and he was young. My mum took a breakdown in the house – the madness that was going on from these bailiffs outside, savages – and he watched her cut her wrists. Years later, he's never really recovered from that; it plays on his mind. He's a very good-looking boy and a lovely person. But there's a distance when you look into his eyes sometimes. He's very vulnerable, very fragile, emotionally he's never been right since that eviction

It was very hard at the time, as he was starting to get his life really together. He'd met a beautiful girl from Canada, Roisin, and she was now pregnant. So he was selling his house in Northern Ireland and he was relocating to Canada, and he'd come over to help me, say his goodbyes and to let me know that his life was going really well.

Anyway, he got dragged into this for no reason. I'd rented a car for him from a friend of mine who worked for a car rental firm and he gave me a really good discount. What I didn't realise was the guy that was working for the rental car firm had been doing mischief and pocketing the money from Six Rental Cars, and he'd pocketed the money from this particular company. Then they arrested him and they charged him for ripping the company off. So, when they went through the files of cars that he'd been hiring to people without putting the money through Six Rental Cars, they found my name hiring one of the cars. Then they realised that this particular car had gone over to Northern Ireland. So the police stopped the car in Northern Ireland. It wasn't a stolen car; it was a rental car that the guy hadn't paid the rental firm for, but it wasn't a stolen car.

Connolly was driving the car in Belfast with my older brother, Emmet, my sister and my brother-in-law – a police officer from New York.

The West Midlands Police had gone over to Northern Ireland and with the RUC had stopped this car in an armed coup on the car, like they were dealing with some sort of terrorists. All of them, including my brother-in-law, the cop, were dragged out of the car and abused, guns put to them, everything else.

First of all, they held Connolly in Belfast and they put him on to the landing of Johnny Adair, who was the top

Loyalist terrorist in Northern Ireland. Here's a young Dublin boy put on to the landing two doors from one of the most dangerous terrorist prisoners, Mad Dog Johnny Adair.

The boy had nothing to do with the crime. We'd proved in court that the rental car had nothing to do with this particular case. But the seeds of doubt had been planted in the jury's heads. The fact that he'd been stopped in the car in Northern Ireland and the fact that he'd been stopped for speeding on his way to the docks in the car before that – they were painted a real nasty picture.

Then they terrorised him by putting him on to the landing with Johnny Adair. Eventually, the British Police went over and brought him over to England. But he'd gone through an ordeal; he didn't want to leave his cell.

While we were in prison, the Crown Prosecution appealed against the sentencing, saying the sentencing was too light, which was rubbish. I've never been in trouble in my life before; I had an honourable discharge from the FCA in Ireland, which is the part-time army; I'd been with Delta Airlines, FAA registered; I'd been a licensee for a pub; and I had no criminal record. It wasn't a violent crime. But they tried to get us seven years. The Crown Prosecution won and ended up getting us an extra 18 months. They didn't go after my brother for extra time because they probably knew in their heart and souls that he was an innocent man.

I had respect amongst the prisoners due to the boxing. I was well known in the Midlands. Blakenhurst Prison is in the Midlands, so a lot of people knew us from the pub because the pub had gained respect amongst people as we'd stood up against these National Front Combat 18 scum, so we'd respect among the black community and we'd respect amongst the honourable criminals, if there is such a thing as an honourable criminal.

The time passed quietly. It's a very strict, monitored regime, so it was very difficult – even going to the gym, you had to put your name down. Anything that you had to do was closely monitored. It was very, very strict – it was a prison – you're limited to what you can do. I didn't see much bullying going on. I'm sure there was bits of bullying going on, but because you're confined to your cell you don't see.

It was monotonous and dragged out. We had a TV in our cell, which helped to pass the time. We watched television. You got the newspaper, two newspapers per landing, so you'd get a certain amount of time to look at the newspaper. So, when the newspaper was given into your cell, you read every piece of the newspaper just to pass the time. You'd read even the advertisements.

You had two visits a month for an hour, and you weren't allowed to touch.

After about four or five months, we got shipped out to a Category D prison because our crime wasn't a violent crime. So we ended up in Leyhill Prison, which was down in Gloucester. It was an open prison and it was nice to be able to walk around and not have a cell locked behind you. It was strange because we weren't in a cell, it was more like a room. We were given a room key. There were rugby pitches, football pitches, tennis courts, and – as far as a prison goes – it had nice facilities, nice conditions. But you've earned it to get to here, you've conducted yourself properly in the other prisons; you'd got your Category D which meant that you were a low risk. It was nice to be able to be in that environment rather than being locked up 23 hours a day. So I appreciated being in that environment and Connolly's room was next door to mine.

AIR FORCE ONE

But in Leyhill I saw a lot of bullying.

There was the rugby team in Leyhill. Gloucester is close to Wales, so there was a lot of Welsh prisoners in Leyhill because they'd come from Gloucester Jail and in Wales rugby is a big game. The Leyhill rugby team were in the league; of course, they couldn't play 'away' games, but teams from the league would come to play them at the prison. Every couple of weeks, there was a rugby game. And it was good to go up and watch because it passed a few hours. But there was a lot of attitude amongst the Leyhill rugby squad. There was a lot of testosterone and a lot of attitude. They walked around, they had that 'kick sand in your face' attitude. So I didn't carry the same respect in Leyhill that I carried in Blakenhurst because I wasn't known as such at Leyhill, which is way out of the Midlands.

I was small compared to some of the rugby players. Some of them were massive men. And there was one particular rugby guy they all called 'Killer' because he'd killed a man on the rugby pitch. There was a row, he punched another player and killed him.

He was a very, very aggressive rugby player. Passionate obviously about the game, but aggressive and that's what he was in prison for. But there was a lot of attitude within the prison. The attitude, the strength of these guys, whatever, they had the attitude. But at least we were out from 7.45 in the morning to 8.45 at night. You were out of your room, as such, and you were able to walk the grounds. You had to go to your prison jobs. They had what's called a tally four times a day. Quarter to eight in the morning, you had to be in your room, they'd come round and check. At quarter to twelve, you had to be in your room. At quarter to five and nine o'clock, you had to be in your room. You could read or watch television in your room. Some of the rooms had televisions, but not all of them. We were over on one side of the building. After nine o'clock, you couldn't go to the other side of the building. There were two TV lounges our side of the building and two TV lounges the other side of the building. Each of the TV lounges had a designated TV channel. So you watched that. If you wanted ITV, you'd go to one room, the other for BBC.

It was fair. But, after nine o'clock, because there was only two rooms we had access to, there was sometimes a little bit of friction over who wanted to watch what. It was OK the way it was done. But I didn't go in there much; I spent most of my time writing letters and stuff. I'm not really a television person. I'm a film man, I like watching films.

So I wasn't in the TV lounge that much because the documentaries and the soaps don't appeal to me. But this particular night my brother asked me if I wanted to come down and watch this film, *Air Force One*. Gary Oldman's in the film and the one from *Raiders of the Lost Ark*. So I said, 'I've seen the film, Connolly, loads of times.'

Anyway, Connolly for some reason insisted on me coming down to watch the film. I thought to myself, 'Well, he's insisting that I go down, so I'll go down.' So, as I'm on my way down to watch the film, there was a lot of lads who wanted to watch the film standing outside this TV room. There's small insignificant guys and one particular guy we'd nicknamed Joe 90 because he looked like him, but not bullying him by calling him Joe.

So I walked past them and there's eight or nine of the rugby team in this particular TV room. Now most of the time they were upstairs in the other TV room because Killer, one of the rugby guys, was on the landing upstairs and a lot of the rugby guys used to congregate on his landing. He seemed to have more respect among the rugby players because of his rugby aggression, his passion for the game, whatever reason. But, when I walked into the TV room, Killer's sitting in this particular TV room which was strange with seven or eight other rugby players.

So, as I walked in, I said, 'How's it going, Killer? Are you watching the film?'

He said, 'No, the snooker's on.' It was the night that Peter Ebdon was playing Stephen Hendry in the final.

I said, 'Oh, there's a good movie on.'

And Killer looked at me and he said, 'I've just told you the snooker's on.'

I thought to myself, 'Say nothing.' I'd earned being in Category D. I'm not saying I'm enjoying my sentence, but I'm enjoying this particular prison a lot more than the lock-up. So I thought, 'Over a TV film? No, I'll walk out.' So I turned and I said, 'No problem, lads.'

As I'm walking out, there's the group of insignificant guys that I've come past. As I'm walking out, I could see in their faces that they couldn't understand why the big man was walking out. Connolly's obviously told these young lads that his big brother Joe is going to get the film put on for them. And he's now wondering why his brother, who in his eyes is a tough guy, is walking out. It's not like me.

So Connolly said, 'What are you doing, Joe?'

'Ah, they're watching the snooker, Connolly, leave them to it.'

'No, we all want to watch the film, there's a load of us want to watch the film.'

'Sorry, lads, let them watch their snooker.'

'Joe, the snooker's on upstairs as well. Half of them are cheering Ebdon and half of them are cheering Hendry. They've got both rooms.'

'What! They're watching the snooker upstairs as well?'

'Yeah. They've took both rooms. They've put us all out.'

'Ah. I'm not having that.'

So I turned and I walked back in. I walked to the television and I switched the television over. I turned and I looked at Killer. 'The film's on. You got a problem with that? If you haven't got a problem, just get out. If you've got a problem, stand your ground.'

And he looked and I could see the blood drain out of his face. Because I thought to myself, 'If he says anything, I'll just cave his face in where he sits.' Even if he'd attempted to stand up, I would have shafted him. Whether I would have took the rest of them, I don't know, but I knew I was going to cave him in. Now this is a man that has killed a man on the rugby pitch. But I don't like bullying. He bullied me so that I had to walk out; I'd swallowed my pride and I walked out. But now he'd bullied a group of insignificant guys and my younger brother.

I'm standing over him. And I thought to myself, 'If he makes even an attempt...' I've been in a lot of situations where I've had to look men in the eyes, and he didn't want to look; he didn't want the eye contact. He hadn't got the heart for the fight. So I'm looking down at Killer, I'm standing over him. And he's looking up at me, and then he eventually looks down. And I could see the rest of the rugby team sitting behind him and they're all waiting for him to make his move. When he looks down, I knew then he was a beaten man. I knew then the fight had gone out of him.

So I stepped back. 'Are you going?' I said. 'Get out.'

He stands up, puts his head in his chest and he walks out. I looked at the rest of them. 'The rest of yous, out. Out now.' And the rest of them stood up, head on chest, walked out single file, like a herd of sheep. Next of all, Joe 90, Connolly and all these insignificant guys filled the room and you could see them all buzzing because the bullies had been put out. They walk in and they sit down.

Air Force One goes on. So I sit down for a couple of minutes and then I just leave them to watch the film.

After that, no problem, no problem whatsoever!

GYM BULLIES

Normally, when you went to the gym, you had all these weight lifters and power lifters. They're the ones with first access to the weights.

I've gone up to the gym and me and my brother were training in the gym. And the weight lifters and the rugby team seemed to have full control of the weights, the machines and everything else. So you had to sort of wait your turn for these guys to finish.

So, anyway, me and Connolly were up there and there was two of the power lifter guys, they weren't the rugby team, but they were the big muscle-barons. They had a load of weights all round them on this particular bench. So I picked up the weights that I could use because there wasn't much left, they had it all. An octopus wouldn't lift the weights that they were lifting. They'd sets of weights all around them. You've only got one set of arms, so you can only use two weights at a time, and they'd got six sets of weights all around them. So there was 12 prisoners that couldn't use anything while these guys had all these weights around them, these muscle-barons. So I picked up two of the weights that were there, but Connolly couldn't lift these weights, as they were a bit too heavy for him.

So he looked across and he said, 'Them ones there, Joe, I can lift.'

I said, 'Well, them lads aren't using them. Ask them if we can use the weights.'

So Connolly walked over and he said, 'Excuse me, can we use these particular weights?'

They said, 'We're using them.'

So he walked back.

I said, 'What's wrong?'

'They said they're using them.'

'They're not using the weights; they're nowhere near using the weights. They're using the other weights.' They've got these sitting at their feet; they will eventually use them, but they're not using them now. So I said, 'They're not using them. Go and ask them again, can you use the weights.'

So Connolly walked over. I was standing near watching. He said, 'Lads, you're not using the weights, can I use them?'

'I've just told you, haven't I? We're using the weights.'

So I stepped in. They're bigger than me, they're full of their muscles and their steroids. I said, 'You've just told him, have you? I'll tell *you*. See you, I will rip your arms clean out of your body. I will smash you to bits with your own arms. He's using them weights, OK? You got a problem with that?'

And his balls dropped. The fact that I'd got the courage to stand up to him, his balls dropped, he didn't want to know. And he says, 'No, no, no problem. I don't want any trouble.'

So I said, 'Connolly, take whatever weights that you want.' I looked around. I said, 'The rest of you lads that are waiting, you take whatever weights you want as well.'

And they came in.

I said, 'You pair, go over there. Stand over there and do your weights over there. These lads are all going to use this position here now.'

And all the lads that were standing there waiting like sheep to use these particular weights then walked over and they used the weights. They were bullying. I didn't want any confrontation with anybody, but you can't stand idly by, especially with your brother.

I'M NOT GOING TO VOMIT IN ANY MAN'S CAR!

While I was in prison, one of the prison officers, Mr Higgins, had a heart attack. I'd been in the St John Ambulance and I knew a bit about First Aid, so I attended to him. He was an OSG officer – old guys doing a bit of part-time work helping in the prisons.

I massaged his chest, kept him calm till the other officers came along, and said an ambulance was on its way. The senior prison officer said, 'Right, you'll get a commendation off the governor for aiding Mr Higgins.'

When I got into the open prison, I got involved with the Windsor Project which was to help the community and also get the message across that all prisoners weren't bad, how we weren't paedophiles, we weren't rapists, and that some of us were ordinary people that just turned the wrong corner and we needed a second chance. I got a commendation for the Windsor Project.

I went out to speak to Job Centres. I went out to speak

to potential bosses, to give prisoners a second chance. I did OK under the work out scheme, and I got my parole on the first attempt.

I served two years. The court battle went on for 18 months because I wasn't well so I genuinely couldn't go to court. I couldn't sit for a long time.

I was very, very sick, my weight was dropping. Even though I'm big, I was gaunt and I had yellow jaundice. I was very, very ill.

While I was in prison, the doctors told me that, because I'd had the abscesses cut out of me, there was a possibility that the abscesses might come back.

This day I was in the showers washing myself and I felt a lump in my back passage where I'd had an abscess cut out before. I felt sick because I thought, 'Oh, Jesus, they're back.' When you get the abscess cut out of your back passage, they don't stitch the wound, they kind of pack it instead. And I didn't want this again. So I was panicking.

I contacted the senior officer who was on duty. He was the same senior officer who had seen how I'd helped Mr Higgins. Straight away, he checked my medical forms on the computer and saw that there was a possibility of abscesses. He took me to the local hospital that night. When the nurse touched the abscess, I spun around: 'Ahhhh!' with the pain. The officer heard the scream from the other room.

She said, 'Yeah, it's an abscess.' She could see it sticking out.

On our way back in the car to Leyhill Prison, I said to the prison officer, 'I feel sick, you'll have to stop.'

It was a genuine man who took me to the hospital. I'm not talking about a prison officer; I'm talking about a man who took me to the hospital on his own back. He knew that I was genuinely ill. He went against whatever authority, he took it on his own.

So there I am, projectile vomiting outside the car. I got back into the car.

He said to me, 'Thank you for not vomiting in my car.'

It wasn't a prison car, it was his own car!

I said, 'I wouldn't do that to any man, especially not a man that's just prepared to put his neck on the chopping block to help me.'

Next day, anyway, I was taken to the hospital and it turned out that it wasn't another abscess, it was combust piles! But it was a relief, yeah, a very big relief.

I'M NOT A GANGSTER'S MOLL!

Ruth doesn't want to be seen as a Florence Nightingale, even though she did clean up blood, sick and shit, after me being sick. She says she doesn't want to see Lisa portrayed as a glamour model and her portrayed as a skivvy!

She has got a good heart and she's a girl that has stood by me.

When I had to get rid of the Lyndhurst pub, I put the money that I'd saved and the money that I'd got from the Lyndhurst and everything else into taking over the Moseley Arms. Now the Moseley Arms was in a derelict condition when we took it over. We spent three months gutting the place and we got the pub to where it was beautiful. At that stage, over the period of three months putting money into it, it wasn't looking good in the court battle, and it was looking like I'm going to prison.

So I've said to Ruth, 'I can't run this pub if I'm in prison. All my money is gone. All our money has gone into this pub.'

At the time, Ruth was working with the Halifax. She's a professional woman, a career woman. Her sister, Lisa, is a senior bank manager and her other sister is a senior psychiatric matron. There's the three girls. So she had a good job in the Halifax estate agents, and she'd worked for them for four and a half years and she was working her way up to become the mortgage adviser. Anyway, she had prospects, a career. She'd worked part-time in the pub and she'd worked part-time as a barmaid in her teenage years, so she knew a little bit about working in the pub. And, when I asked her, she took her redundancy from the Halifax to come and run the Moseley Arms, and she became the licensee.

And, if she hadn't, everything I put into that pub would have been gone because, nine days after opening the Moseley Arms, I was sent to prison and Ruth was thrown in at the deep end.

Not only was she put in to run a business when she'd only really been a barmaid, now she's having to run a pub with her other half going to prison.

So she's took a nervous breakdown as a result of everything that's happened to her and she forced herself to get better. Her weight plummeted from 10 stone to below 7 stone.

I remember the day she came to visit me in prison, and

Tommy, my business partner, was in the visits hall. Prison visits rules were you're not supposed to move from your table, so he'd no business doing this, but he walked all the way across the visits room. A couple of prison officers were screaming at him and he came over and he gave Ruth a hug.

He looked at me and he said, 'What have you done to this girl?'

And I was feeling guilty enough; I didn't need him to work it into me. But he was that concerned.

And he said to her, 'Come on, get yourself together. You'll be all right.'

She pulled her way out. She kept it together and she ran the Moseley Arms. For the two years I was in prison, she ran and built that pub. She's got a great strength of character about her and she's a very private person.

She kept the pub going, my friends gave her a hand and kept supporting her and everything else and the business went from strength to strength.

The Moseley Arms pub was beside a police station in Digbeth. The police used to frequent the pub regularly. But they stopped frequenting the pub and they came in and said to Ruth, 'We won't come into this pub now any more because you're a front for a gangster.'

And Ruth told them, she said, 'How many gangster's molls do you know that clean toilets? How many gangster's molls do you know that scrub floors, that clean the windows. I'm not a gangster's moll, I'm a hard-working woman. And Joe's no gangster. He was a hard-working man until you caused him all those problems.

It's true. If they'd stood by me the first time round I wouldn't have had them.

I got out of prison in 2003. My parole finished in November 2004. Ruth was running the pub. And I have a man's pride and ego, you know, you want to earn your own money, but my licence has gone now because I've got the criminal record.

I'd left school very young, the only thing I'd ever done was box. Like I said in the beginning, everything I'd ever done was for boxing. The only time in my life I'd ever been totally content was when I was boxing. Now suddenly, when I'm outside of boxing, everything's not going right. But every door I knocked on to try and get something for work, there was nothing happening.

So I decide to make a comeback in the boxing for the first time in 12 years.

'JOE, YOU CUT THAT FINE!'

I've now gone from being Joe the boxer to Joe the publican to Joe the convict, and now I'm back to Joe the boxer again, and it's nice for people to talk about me for the boxing once more.

So I'm out of prison, and I'm training. One day, when me and my training partner, Patrick, finish training, we go for something to eat. So, we go to this place on Broad Street that does these magnificent chicken breasts. Patrick owns a pub in Digbeth called Cleary's and there's a guy called Lee Marshall, who is the veteran world's strongest man, who sometimes does the door for him. Lee's won over 40 strong-man titles. So we're getting these breasts of chicken and Lee is on the door of the Rocket Club, and he spots Patrick and we're chatting away. And I'm congratulating Lee, who's just won his seventh world veterans title.

Les Cole, the manager, steps out. 'Joe Egan!' And he gives me a big hug because I've just been out of prison. 'Come in, come in!'

'Les, I've just finished training; I'm just having a bit of chicken.

He starts to pull my arm.

I say, 'Les, I'll come up another time.' I say to Lee, 'Lee, I won't even attempt to wrestle with you, you'll pull my arm out of its socket! I will come up again. Here's my number, Les.'

So, the next day, Les rings me. 'Joe, we're having a medal presentation for Lee for winning his seventh world power lifting title. The newspapers are going to be there. Will you come to the medal presentation and be a celebrity in the photograph.'

I said, 'I will by all means, no problem.'

So I organised a few boxing friends to come up for the photograph. It's a lap-dancing club, but it's a free bar; there's girls dancing, but the Irish lads just want to have the drink. So I'm standing there talking with Les about what's happening, things like that. The press are there and they take the photographs. I was having an orange juice at the bar and I spot Michael Flatley, in the audience, in the crowd.

Michael Flatley!

Security all come running over. 'Joe, Joe, it's not Michael Flatley, it's only his lookalike.'

I walk over and I swear to God he is the spit of Michael Flatley.

And he also *is* Michael Flatley, because he's actually changed his name by Deed Poll to Michael Flatley! He drives around with his registration on his Mercedes, Flatley. His gold card, Visa card, driving licence – it's all been changed to Michael Flatley.

On two occasions, he's been down to Flatley's changing rooms at Flatley's concerts, and got through all the security! He's been ushered into venues as Flatley because he's the double of him.

I hadn't been aware of this guy.

So now I'm in the presence of Michael Flatley's double, his lookalike. But I'm looking and I'm still shaking my head, is it Michael Flatley?

So I go over to talk to him.

He says, 'I'm Richard from Stowport, I've changed my name, I'm not the real Michael Flatley. I've been trying to get to meet you, but you've been in prison. Paddy Finn and Mike Higgins have been trying to get a meeting on with you.'

And I'm listening to this Stowport accent so I know. But I'm still in shock because it's his double.

I say, 'You want to do me a favour?'

'Anything.'

'Right, I'm going to walk away now, but do you see that group of lads over there?'

'Yeah.'

'Go over and sit beside them. They're my friends. I won't let anything happen to you. As soon as they realise what's going on, I'll go over and I'll stop them before they do anything.'

'Promise?'

'I promise.'

So I'm standing back. The lads are all laughing and drinking because it's a free bar. The Irish lads are all wanting the gargle. There's Patrick and Paul and Patrick's uncle Peter, and a couple of other Irish lads.

'Flatley' goes over and, brazen, he sits beside Patrick and looks at him. Patrick goes, 'Aaagghh!' He's looking, all of the other lads are all looking too. There's not a word being said because you can see no lips are moving.

Anyway, the drink's gone down. So, next of all, I can see Richard, he's not saying a word, none of them is saying a word. And you know the headbutt's coming.

Then I walk over, I put my hand on Patrick's chest. Richard's face would have been smashed. I said, 'It's all right, he's not the real man!'

Richard goes, 'Joe, you cut that fine.'

CHAPTER TEN

Comeback

'JOE! YOU'RE MISSING THE STEPS!'

I'd been a character witness for Mike Tyson in his rape case with Desiree Washington – I'd sent a letter to Judge Patricia Gifford, about my time I spent with Mike and how I found him as a person. So I've been there in Mike's time of need. I had a lovely letter back from Tyson's people acknowledging the letter and thanking me for my help.

So I contacted Tyson. Not asking cap in hand, I've never gone cap in hand to anybody. I just asked him if I could do some work, be his sparring partner, anything.

Right away, he said, if I wanted to come over, he would help me get back on track. I wasn't asking for any handout. I could ask Mike Tyson for anything and that man would give me anything, I know. He's a very generous man. But I've never asked him for anything. I asked him for help and he's there for me.

He said, 'Boxing on my undercard?'

So I said, 'Yeah, OK.'

I'd been 12 years out of the ring! I thought, 'Well, I don't want to take a fight on his undercard and embarrass myself. I'll take a warm-up fight.'

And I also thought, 'What better place to take a warm-up fight than at home in Ireland, because I'll get the true opinion.' In England, you're going to get people saying, 'Great, you look great, brilliant,' when you look shit.

But I thought, 'If I go home, and look like shit, the Irish are going to tell me, "You look shit."' Sometimes the reality hurts, but they give it to you. If you're not up to it, they'll tell you.

So I get a fight in Dublin.

I'm training hard. I'm sparring with Steven Petitt, former Midlands area champion, and Nigel Rafferty, another former Midlands champion, who had over 100 pro fights. Two good fighters. I have no manager, I'm just self-managed. I'm using Flex Fitness Gym in Digbeth, which is owned by Saleem 'Sal' Raza, an Asian guy. It's a lovely gym. There's a lot of boxers train there.

I'm moving well, sparring well. Christian Brady's taking me on the pads. Patrick Naughton's working with me on the weights. Because I'm building myself up, I've got myself into good shape.

So there's a great interest now at home and, because of the carry on with Flatley, they're billing me now as the 'Lord of the Ring', where he was the Lord of the Dance. The Irish newspapers thought this joke fight was a big issue. I thought, 'I've got his angle.' He challenged me first time round when I was on my sick bed.

When they did the press conference in Ireland for the fight, Steve Collins hosted the press conference, and someone in the audience from the Irish newspapers asked, 'Is it true you've challenged Flatley?'

Gerry Callan from the *Irish Daily Star* interrupted and said, 'Joe hasn't challenged Michael Flatley. Joe's responding to Michael Flatley's original challenge. Flatley challenged Joe first time round.'

'That's right,' I said. 'He challenged me first time round when I was on my sick bed. Now I'm back, I'm fit and healthy. I'll accept any challenge that he's got. Anything he wants, I'll fight him.'

The guy that I fought is a good friend, Mark Williams. I'd trained with Mark and I'd sparred with him a number of years before. I'd got him ready for two of his pro fights, two good wins – one in Barking and one in Ipswich. And Mark hadn't boxed for two years. He received a gunshot wound to the stomach and the British Boxing Board of Control were giving him a bit of a hard time over his licence. So it was beneficial to us both; it was going to get him back on track after two years, and me after 12 years. We weren't there to kill each other, we were there to give a good show. But it's like anything else, a man's pride. You want to get in and you want to give a good display.

And it was an opportunity for him to prove to the British Boxing Board of Control that he was still capable of fighting, even though he'd had that gunshot to the stomach.

I asked Tony Mahon, for nostalgia, for old time's sake. Paul McCullagh and John Breen had been my cornermen and trainers when I'd been a pro, but Tony had been there when I was an amateur. I was back in Dublin and it was my comeback so I asked Tony if he would do me the honour of doing my corner, and he said yes.

Now I used to come into Irish music. The Fureys, 'The Lonesome Boatman', because it's a lonesome place, the boxing ring. But, after what happened with Flatley and Lisa, I thought, 'Oh, stuff this Irish music, I'm not coming in to any Irish music.'

So I spent literally hours picking out a bit of music to come in to. But my friend Steve's missus, Anna, has choreographed different stage shows and stuff, so she knows her music, and we picked out different songs and eventually chose one by the American rap band The Fugees: 'Ready or not, here I come, you can't hide.'

I'm in the changing rooms; I'm getting bandaged up, and there's a nice atmosphere. My two old trainers, John Breen and Paul McCullagh, had fighters on the undercard of the bill. Brendan Ingle, Prince Naseem Hamed's old trainer, had a fighter on the card, so there was a lovely buzz in the changing rooms. So I'm nice and relaxed, and there's friends I haven't seen for a long time.

We were boxing in the Burlington Hotel. And there was a lovely atmosphere. I'd been interviewed for the Irish television channel. I was a bit nervous, but I rested during the day, had a bit of food and I'm nice and calm – even though it's 12 years out of the ring. At that moment in time, I'd forgotten what the fear was like. So I'm nice and calm, and John Breen is bandaging my hands.

Darren Corbett, from Belfast, who's been the Commonwealth cruiserweight champion, great fighter, great puncher, comes in to wish me luck and talk to me and stuff. He says, 'Joe, the guy you're fighting is in the next room, scream and shout, go mad. Aaaahhhhh!'

I'm relaxed, laughing. I said, 'Darren, I can't do that, it's not me, trying to put the fear in my opponent.'

The inspector examined my bandages and put the stamp on my hand. I glove up, and I'm nice and calm. They say, 'Right, Joe, make your way to the ring.'

Then I swear to God, my legs froze. I froze. I nearly fell forward; my legs wouldn't move. The music, may God strike me down, the music blasting from the changing rooms to the ring, I didn't hear it, because of the fear. Twelve years and I'd forgotten what the fear was like.

I walked to the ring, towards the steps, and I walked right on by the steps.

One of the spectators at ringside calls out, 'Joe! You've missed the steps!'

I stop. Oh, yeah. I turn back and climb into the ring. If that person hadn't called out, I would have walked right out of the building and got to my mum's front door with my boxing gloves on. Let me in! I didn't want to be there.

So I climb up into the ring and I see Mark. Mark Williams is a very, very impressive-looking man, and he's an impressive-looking man that can fight. I've sparred with him and he's as tough a man as I know. He's unfortunate with the fact that his management don't get him the opportunities that he should have in the boxing. He's a better fighter than his record because he's taken fights at short notice. He'd only been inactive for two years because of the gunshot wound.

The fight's billed as a six rounder. The first two rounds

he's a lot sharper, lighter, faster, and he's giving me a bit of a pasting. It's two years out of the ring for him, 12 years for me. He's younger than me, and lighter than me.

I've boxed at a better level than Mark, amateur and professional, but he's fought at a good level as a pro. He's sharp, he's fast, he's fit, he's strong, he's catching me with some good shots.

At the end of round one, I go back to the corner and whatever my thought was before the bell went about not wanting to be there, at the end of round one I *definitely didn't* want to be there!

Tony gives me a slap into the face, a thump. 'Will you wake up!' It wasn't asleep I was, but rusty. 'Come on! Get it together!'

So up for round two and the same thing again, another round one.

I go back to the corner and Tony's giving me another pep talk. 'Will you wake up! He's slaughtering you!'

Next round, round three, I started to get it together and we had a good bit of toe-to-toe. Then round four, I started to get a bit more together.

And now my strength – I'm stronger than Mark only in the fact that I'm heavier – starts to get the better. He'd given it out for the first two rounds, now he was taking it for round three and four.

In round four, I jolted him as I tried to pull him into a corner. I wanted to keep him in the corner, I didn't want him moving, as he was too fast and graceful. And whatever way I pushed him in the corner, I've sort of jerked his shoulder. At the end of the round, I'm looking across, because you want to see what injuries they've got, and the ref was over with him, and I could see him complaining about his shoulder.

True warrior that he was, he came out for round five. But the pain in his shoulder was too much and he had to retire in round five.

It was a good fight, and Mark Williams gave as good as he got. At that stage I wouldn't like to pick it on points because he'd won the first two rounds, I'd won the second two rounds. We weren't much into round five, so there wasn't much of a difference on points. I won on a TKO, technical knock out, but it wasn't for anything other than his shoulder.

But it doesn't matter what way you win!

I was leaping around.

Funnily enough, there were two brothers in opposite corners. I had my friend Patrick Naughton in my corner with Tony Mahon, and his brother Paul Naughton was in the opposite corner with Mark Williams's trainer, Dave Lovell, who was a good pro. So there all my friends.

I embraced all the cornermen, the fighter, the trainers, and then I wanted to see Ruth. So I'm on the ring apron shouting, 'Ruth! Ruth!' – it was like the *Rocky* movie when he's shouting 'Adrian!' So I'm shouting, and she's outside with the mobile phone, obviously ringing around. So, as I stepped down off the ring apron, all my friends – because I only live down the road from the Burlington – my friends and my family and stuff they're all giving me hugs and kisses and embraces.

Top of the world!

HEADACHE!

But after the fight I had the headache from hell. Unbelievable.

Men joke about it when the women say, 'Oh not tonight, I've got a headache.'

I'd been over in Ireland doing the press conferences for the fight and in the final week for the training, so I hadn't seen Ruth for nearly two weeks. Now being at the boxing, for a lot of women, it's a form of foreplay because it's like two gladiators.

So she's all excited. We go up to the hotel room, get showered and come back down to the party. My head is thumping but I have to see the friends, the family, the people who've come to support me; it was brilliant. Ruth's having a drink of wine.

When we went back up to our hotel room, Ruth was a bit frisky. And I said, 'Oh, Ruth, my head is thumping, and I mean thumping.'

I was boxing on 30 May and she'd turned 30 on 5 May. And it's a big step for women turning 30, and she was just feeling a little bit frisky after the fight. But my headache was really, really bad. I'd taken a good few shots. My head was thumping.

I said, 'Ruth, my head.'

'Oh, it's because I'm 30 now, you're going off me'!

'No, Ruth!'

'Oh, you don't want me. I'm 30!'

'Ruth, please, please!'

I ended up having to go down and sit in the lobby of the hotel. Two hours earlier, I'm the hero, now I'm sitting in the lobby like a lost soul, my head thumping, everybody's gone.

After an hour or whatever, I went back up, and she's asleep so I went to bed and I cuddled her.

The next morning the headache was gone!

But now, if Ruth says to me, 'I have a headache,' I respect it. I don't push the issue!

MY DADDY'S THE TOUGHEST GUY ON THE PLANET!

In my comeback fight, I was a bit rusty. Twelve years out of the ring's a long time. But I stopped him in the fifth, and I had a big write-up in the *Boxing News*. 'George Forman makes the comeback after 10 years, Big Joe Egan makes the comeback after 12 years.'

It was lovely. Even to be mentioned in the same write-up as George was great, because George is one of the living legends. So to get a mention in the same write-up as George Forman was an honour.

After the fight, I'm speaking to Brendan Ingle, 'Prince' Naseem Hamed's ex-manager, who had a fighter on the bill, and I said, 'How did I look?'

'You looked all right.'

I had a brain scan afterwards, and I had a brain scan before. They insist on it, you've got to go and get it done straight away. It was OK. It had to be, because my plan was to go over and fight on Tyson's undercard when he fought Kevin McBride.

So I contacted Tyson, and I contacted Showtime. I said, 'I've had a good result, I've had a win. I feel good. I didn't look too bad. I'll box on your undercard when you fight Kevin McBride, it'll be great.'

I'm at home and I'm getting my passport all organised, and, while I was at home, I'm stopping with one of my closest friends from old, Steve Dawson, who's an ex-amateur boxing champion. We sparred together on a number of occasions. We used to go and do the exhibition fights before we went working on the doors. And you get yourselves some money rather than a trophy and then you go work the doors, so you'd have double the money for a night's work. And it was great.

Anyway, I'm staying in his house with his missus and his son, Tristan. And I was getting ready for the fight in America. I'm buzzing, and everything's going great. And Steve says, 'We'll go round the gym, do a bit of training.'

'Right.'

'We'll do some sparring.'

'You haven't boxed in years!'

'Neither have you! You've only had the one fight in 12 bloody years!'

'OK.'

It's like old times! Apollo Creed and Rocky go back to the gym after all those years. It was exactly what it was like.

Anyway, we're leaving the house and Tristan says, 'Are you and Daddy going to box?'

I say, 'Yeah.'

'Who's the toughest?'

'Oh, your daddy's the toughest man on the planet.'

So we went down to Phil Sutcliffe's gym. And we're in the ring, headgear on, sparring gloves. My heart's racing because it's like we haven't done it for years and years, we haven't shared a boxing ring for years. So I'm buzzing, and he's buzzing. We've been training together, like jogging, skipping and stuff. He's helped me get into good shape. But now we're doing a bit of sparring.

So, next thing, I ducked and he caught me an uppercut. The punch wasn't anything; it was like a stinging punch, a glancing punch. I had the headgear on and it just caught the eye and I felt the blood running down my face and I just stopped.

He said, 'Are you OK?'

I said, 'Sorry, Steve.'

'Oh, Joe.'

And next I just felt the blood running down my face. I took the headgear off and he'd split my eye. And it was on the bone, it was a good rip. It wasn't even the best of punches; it was a good crisp shot, but it just split me. It was a good shot, but he'd caught me with better shots over the years.

And I thought to myself, 'Well, if he can do that with a friendly punch, how much damage is a man going to do with a bad-intentions punch?' I am too old now to be getting wounds like that. You don't heal as quick the older you get. And I thought at the same moment, 'No I don't need this, I've already got a good job now, I've landed a good job.' Different doors were starting to open for me again. The desire wasn't there as what it was two months earlier.

We went to the hospital, three stitches were put in and my eye was swollen up a little bit.

There was the talk that Tyson wasn't going to be fighting McBride, so there wasn't the same buzz of anticipation with the Irish connection, so that was a bit of a dampener on it as well. But, at the time, the Danny Williams fight hadn't been announced. Tyson versus McBride was still possible. If they asked me, I would have to say no. My eye was bad, and I wouldn't have been ready.

We got back to Steve's house and the first person to meet us at the front door was his little boy. And he sees my eye. 'Oh, what happened to your eye?'

'Well, your daddy cut me when we were boxing.'

'Oh, you said he was the toughest man on the planet!'

At that moment, we laughed, but it was, you know, one of those nervous tension laughs. I was laughing and me and Steve just gave him a big hug.

Steve's one of my closest friends. The punch wasn't thrown to rip my eye open, or with bad intentions like when you're in a proper fight. It was a sparring session, and he just caught me. And we laughed about it.

But I knew then it was over.

Different people have spoken to me since about fighting again, but I knew at that moment, there and then, at Steve Dawson's front door in Clontarf, with a five-year-old boy looking at my eye, saying, 'You said my daddy was the toughest man on the planet!'

And at that moment on the doorstep when we laughed – the nervous tension laugh – believe it or believe it not, at that moment in time, I felt like the weight of the world was suddenly off my shoulders. I've come back after 12 years and I've had a good win. I've nothing else to prove to anybody.

I've nothing else to prove to myself.

Epilogue

THE GENTLE SIDE

When Mike was charged with the rape of Desiree Washington, I was boxing professional with Barney Eastwood, Barry McGuigan's old manager. He was also one of the biggest bookmakers in Ireland, so, having a bookmaker's licence, he was held in very high regard, a pillar of the community. And I was boxing for him, so I felt that I was a pillar of the community too.

I'd never got in trouble with the police before. I was ex-Irish army, honourable discharge, Delta airlines FAA registered, Federal Aviation Authority registered. I was with Delta for two and a half years. And, when Jay mentioned to me what was happening with Mike, I already knew because it was all over the world news.

And I said, 'Mike's my friend, I think the world of him, I love the man like family, can I do anything to help?'

And Jay said, 'Well, you might be able to put into

words how you find Mike. Do you think it's in his character to do something like this?'

And I said, 'No, I don't think it's in his character to do something like this.'

I wasn't there at the time. He was charged and convicted, but I still believe in my heart of hearts that he didn't do it. The only two people in the world that know are him and Desiree Washington. They were the only two people that were there.

But I believe, from the Mike Tyson that I know, that he didn't do it.

Anyway, I put into words how I found Mike as a person, my time that I spent in the Catskills with Mike, the relationship that I saw that he had with his girlfriend at the time I was there, a girl called Angie. I saw this separate to the sparring, his training, which was very, very intense, the ferocity of the sparring and the ferocity in the fight.

I saw the gentler side of Mike Tyson. I saw the friend Mike Tyson. So I've seen both sides of Mike Tyson. I've seen him in the rage when he's sparring, I've seen him in the rage when he's fighting, and he gets himself into fight mode. But I've seen him outside the ring.

There's the two sides, and the Mike Tyson that I was asked to talk about was the Mike Tyson outside of the fighting ring, outside of the sparring. And he's a genuine lovely man. He's a gentle man – to watch him handling a pigeon, the most powerful man on the planet to be so gentle holding a pigeon. Pigeons are very fragile. He was so gentle, almost timid, holding pigeons.

And I watched him with Angie, the girlfriend he was

with when I first met him, and this man could crush bones. And I'd watch him embrace Angie so gently and tenderly. And I'd watched him embrace Camille, who was an old woman. I'm not saying she was fragile, she was a sturdy woman, but she was an old woman.

That's the side that I tried to put into words and to say how I thought the world of the man. I was hoping that my letter, and I'm sure a lot of other people's letters and stuff that were sent in as character witnesses, was going to help his cause. And I got a lovely letter back from Jay, acknowledging the letter I sent in to forward to the judge, and saying Mike was thanking me for my letter and for my help.

At least I tried.

FANTASTIC GUY

Just before I went back to Dublin to box again after 12 years, I met Gerard Gordon in the barbers. I'd been friends with him for a number of years – he used to frequent the pub with his family, and him and his brother are ex-boxers. He said, 'I'm reading you're boxing again, Joe.'

I said, 'Yeah.'

'You're too old to be boxing. Why are you doing it?'

'What else can I do? I'm hoping that this boxing match will open doors that have become closed because I've gone from Joe the boxer to being Joe the convict, and it doesn't suit me being Joe the convict, it suits me being Joe the boxer.'

'Look, when you come back from Ireland, come and work for me.' He's got four or five different companies –

12 of his company directors came over to Ireland with him to watch the fight. And he bought the gloves that I boxed in for £2,000 for charity. It was fantastic of him.

I came back in June 2004, and I've been working for him ever since.

'YOU DONE GREAT'

Years later, I'm in my new pub with Ruth, and Flatley was getting – it turns out falsely – accused of rape. I'm on a day release from one of the work outs I gave in prison. I'm at home in the pub, and the phone rings. 'Is Joe there? Can I speak to Joe Egan?'

So Ruth takes the call. 'This is such and such a newspaper, we'd like to get a few comments on what Joe thinks of Michael being accused of rape.'

I'm sitting beside her. I didn't know what the call was about. I couldn't hear the other end.

So Ruth says, 'Just leave him alone. That's gone, that's over. The man's in a new relationship. He has no comments to make. Just leave him alone,' and she hangs up.

So I say, 'What was all that about?'

'An Irish newspaper wanted to know if you've got any comments about Flatley,' she said. 'Did I say the right things?'

I said, 'You done great. Well done. You've done great.'

TOUGH GUY

I get invited to a lot of boxing dinners and functions. I've been a guest on different tables, I've been guests at shows with Ricky Hatton and guest at shows with

Thomas Hearns; I've been a guest at shows with Joe Frazier; I've done shows with Steve and Nigel; I've done shows with American Earnie Shavers. I've been all round the countryside.

And Steve's boxing in Dublin, he's defending his title in Dublin against a fighter from Middlesbrough, called Cornelius Carr. Now I'd boxed with Cornelius as an amateur in the North-East Division team, when we'd gone over to Denmark. So Cornelius was my friend and Steve Collins was my friend, so I made every effort to get home to see this particular fight. While I was there, I was lucky to see who the celebrities were at ringside and they'd been all introduced. And at ringside was Nigel Benn, who's my friend, and Scott Welsh who I knew as a heavyweight contender. I'd never met Scott at that stage but I knew Nigel as a friend. Also ringside was Pierce Brosnan, who wasn't James Bond at the time, but he went on to be. He was still a big star, and he'd done a lot of movies.

Anyway, when the fight was over, the inner ringside was opened up and I got through the inner ringside and Steve Collins came over the ring apron. 'Joe Egan,' he shouts. So at that stage Nigel Benn, Pierce Brosnan and Scott Welsh were moving across. So Nigel sees me and acknowledges me; Scott acknowledges me as well and Pierce Brosnan's standing there. So I'm looking at Pierce Brosnan because he's a very, very strikingly handsome man and I'm standing there and I'm looking.

Then I look again at Nigel Benn. He looked very well. He's as tough a man as any man on the planet, Nigel

Benn. But he's got this yellow frilly shirt on. I said, 'Nigel, only a man as tough as you could get away with wearing a shirt like that.'

And Nigel said, 'Joe, only a man as tough as you could get away with a statement like that.'